COMMENTS FROM READERS OF OUR PUBLICATIONS

The following are just a few of the comments from more than seven hundred letters and emails that we have received pertaining to our publications. For additional comments, see our website: lamplight.net.

Trust God for Your Finances

There are more than 150,000 copies of *Trust God for Your Finances* in print. This book has been translated into seven foreign languages.

- "I have translated *Trust God for Your Finances* into Thai. I intended to make about 50 or 60 photocopies of this translation to distribute among friends. My pastor asked for 700 copies to distribute at the special yearly conference for pastors. My immediate thought was that I could not do this, but he urged me to pray and try my best. Surprisingly, it worked out. Thank God. More than 1,000 people attended the conference. Seven hundred copies were distributed to only the pastors, elders and deacons who really wanted the book. After the conference, we had so many calls that another 2,000 copies were printed. Thank you, Mr. Hartman, for this book which is helping so many Thai Christians." (Thailand)

- "I bought your book, *Trust God for Your Finances,* at a church I was attending in Virginia in the 1980s. This book transformed my life. It was all Bible-based and solid in every way. I married a Bulgarian pastor who started the church here during Communism and the underground church. We have pastored together for 22 years. I gave your book to my husband and he consumed it. He kept it near his Bible all the time. God has raised him up to be influential in this nation. He has written a book titled *The Covenant of Provision* dealing with finances. Your book helped him so much to form his ideas about the rightful use of money. This book has influenced my husband more than almost any other book. It was so timely and needed coming out of a Communist society. Thank you so much for this book." (Bulgaria)

- "Today we had a ministry partner join us for lunch. He said that the book, *Trust God for Your Finances*, that we had translated into Hebrew was the most powerful book he had ever read on the subject. I shared with him the wonderful story of how you shared the book with us and how many Israelis have been enlightened in that area as a result of reading the book. You both are a blessing and a treasure in God's kingdom." (Israel)

What Does God Say?

- "Your book *What Does God Say?* is one of the greatest books I have ever read. You tell the truth and back it up with Scripture. I started crime very young. I have spent a large portion of my life behind bars. I have so much to be ashamed of and things that I am very sorry for. I have almost wasted my life. I say almost because this book caused me to realize that God loves even me no matter what I have done. In your book I read that there is no condemnation in Christ Jesus. Do you have any idea what it means to feel no condemnation when society says to lock me up because I am guilty? My sins and all the crimes I have committed have been washed away. I cannot explain how it feels to know that someone is really proud of me. That someone is Jesus. I am taking this book home with me. Even though I don't have much education, I can understand it very well. I now know that I am saved and I am forgiven. Thank you very much for writing this book." (Florida)

- "Several months ago, you sent me a copy of your book titled *What Does God Say?*. This book is amazing. First of all, I could understand it. My English is not great. I have been a Muslim all my life. I was taught as a child what I was supposed to believe. When I was searching for real truth, I met the Master and received Jesus Christ as my Savior. When I read your book, it filled so much of the void and loneliness that I was filled with. I will be sharing Jesus and *What Does God Say?* with my family and with other Muslims. Please pray for me as

I may not be welcomed in my own home town for finding this wonderful Jesus." (Ghana)

- "I am a sixty-two year old retired official in the Royal Thai government. I am a born-again Christian. Throughout my life I think I am a good Christian by going to church. Recently a friend of mine gave me a book titled *What Does God Say?*. At first I thought what could God say to someone like me who prides himself on being a faithful church-goer? When I started reading, however, it was like being awakened from a long sleep. Never before did I know God the way I feel now. I feel so ashamed of being so ignorant all these years thinking that just going to church is enough to be called a good Christian. I don't know how to thank the authors of this book who opened my heart and mind to see God the true way that He is. The remaining years of my life will not be the same with this newfound knowledge of our Savior. Better late than never." (Thailand)

Quiet Confidence in the Lord

- "As soon as I was diagnosed with prostate cancer, I began to meditate on the Scripture and your explanation of the Scripture in *Quiet Confidence in the Lord*. I carried this book with me everywhere for several weeks. The specialist at the Lahey Clinic in Boston told me I was the calmest person with this diagnosis that he had ever seen. During the pre-op and the surgery, a number of people commented on how calm I was. I experienced a lot of discomfort during the difficult first week at home after the surgery. I focused constantly on the Scripture in this wonderful book. I was remarkably calm. Thank you for writing this book that has helped me so much." (Massachusetts)

- "After I graduated from Bible school, I went outside of my country for mission work with my wife. After we were there for nine months, my wife died suddenly. My sorrow was great. I read your book titled *Quiet Confidence in the Lord*. This book spoke to my heart. All twenty-three chapters were written for me. God changed me through this book and comforted me and took away my sorrow. Through the blood of Jesus I entered

God's rest. I can give a great recommendation for this book to anyone who is filled with sorrow and grief. I pray that many people will read this book and develop quiet confidence in the Lord as I did. Thank you so much for sending this book to me. May God bless you and your ministry." (Ethiopia)

- "*Quiet Confidence in the Lord* is with me at work each day. I have read and underlined passages that lift my heart and help me to understand something I've known all along and that is that I am not alone and that God cares very much that I'm in the midst of great adversity. I asked God to send me a comforter, someone who would put their arms around me and say, 'I understand and I care.' The answer to that prayer is in you and Judy. Thanks to *Quiet Confidence of the Lord* I am, for the first time in my life, learning to focus on God and not my problems. Thank you both for your ministry. Your books are a tremendous blessing to hurting people all over the world." (Washington, DC)

Receive Healing from the Lord
- "Your great book, *Receive Healing from the Lord*, has amazed me. This book has been my daily bread. I have followed all of God's instructions in your book. My children and my wife were healed from severe illness. I was sick myself just before an important crusade. I meditated on the Scripture in your book for the entire night. I was totally healed. The following day God did wonders as He healed many people. Since then, people have been coming to receive their healing at our home and church almost every day. Many healings are taking place at our services. This book is wonderful. I am abundantly blessed by it." (Zambia)

- "My husband and I served in the mission field in Swaziland, Africa, for three and a half years. Upon our arrival, Lamplight Ministries sent us four mailbags full of Jack and Judy's books. Because Swaziland is so laden with HIV/AIDS, we were able to use the book, *Receive Healing from the Lord,* with the people in Swaziland to see many people come to a saving knowledge of the Lord Jesus Christ and His perfect will regarding healing. We saw mothers with very sick children who themselves also were afflicted with AIDS respond to the many Scriptures that are part of the book, actually believing that it was meant for them. Had it not been for the use of this book and the other books you sent, we would not have had such success in teaching a Bible study about the truth in God's Word to these people. We gave out your books and told the people that the book was theirs to keep. We saw such joy and surprise on the faces of these impoverished people. We appreciate the ongoing generosity of Lamplight Ministries for 'such a time as this' in these days where there is so much need and want. We will forever be thankful that we can count on the Word of God through the books written by Jack and Judy as effective tools in the transformation of people's lives." (Swaziland)

- "Thank you very much for sending me your book, *Receive Healing from the Lord.* After reading the first chapter I realized that this book could be the solution for my wife's failing health. We decided to read the book together every day. My wife was healed and restored after carefully following the scriptural principles that you explained. We are humbled by how we had struggled and panicked trying to find an answer. God gave us the solution in your book. We are so grateful to you. We love you and we are praying for you." (Zambia)

Effective Prayer
- "I thank God for your book titled *Effective Prayer*. This book came to me at the right time. Since reading this book, God has done great wonders in my life and ministry. Our whole church is being affected by what we have learned about the power of prayer. I have read many books on prayer, but this one is unique. I no longer pray amiss. My prayer life has become much more effective. Your book has helped me to persevere in prayer much longer than before. This is a great book. I love it. I treasure this book. I do not know how to thank you. I pray that God will bless you both with long life and that you will enjoy the fruit of your labour." (Zambia)

- "Your book *Effective Prayer* is a great blessing to me. After reading this book I have so much more understanding about prayer. It is very easy to learn from all that you are teaching and all of the Scriptures in it. I now understand much more about the significance of prayer in my daily life, why I should pray and how to pray. You have enlightened my mind. I know that my loving Father wants me to pray all the time. I have learned to pray God's answer instead of focusing on the problem. This book is very vital to my daily life. I am so thankful to both of you for another great book for people who need answers. Thank you so much for the great understanding that I found in this book." (the Philippines)

- "I have been studying your book *Effective Prayer.* This book has inspired me to do a lot more praying. Praying to God is such a privilege. To know that God is just waiting for me to come and talk with Him is tremendous. The way you brought out the gift of being baptized in the Holy Spirit and praying in tongues will make it easier for people to receive this much-needed gift in their lives. Our pastor is using your book to teach on prayer. I have given copies of this book to many people in our church. I gave one to another pastor in our town. I love you both in the Lord Jesus Christ. I thank God for you and for allowing Him to continue to use you in the body of Christ." (Oklahoma)

What Will Heaven Be Like?
- "On the very first page of your book on heaven I was spellbound. The material read so quickly and coherently that it was like having a conversation with a Christian friend. I could really feel the excitement as we talked about the throne of God and its radiance. Those who are curious about heaven will be so delighted and joyful when they read this book. I think the questions at the end of the book are a great idea. This book is a ready-made classroom treasure. I was deeply moved by the gentle loving approach and the manner this material was presented to me, the reader. I can hardly wait to read your other books. You have gained a new fan and admirer

of your special way of presenting the kingdom of heaven and God's love for us." (Mississippi)

- "I came to China from Cambodia where I was a captain in the army. I was a Buddhist. Four weeks before I came to China, I had a dream where Jesus appeared to me. When I woke up the following morning, I looked for Christians to explain more about Jesus Christ to me. After I came to China, I met a Christian man who gave me the book *What Will Heaven Be Like?*. This book answered many questions for me. My English is not very good, but this book is written in very simple English. I have found new life through this book. Please pray for me so that I can share Jesus with my parents and my Buddhist friends when I go back to Cambodia." (China)

- "I am the Youth Director of our church and I'm leading a group of high school students in a Bible study of your book on heaven. We all respect your opinions and have found your book to be an excellent springboard for discussion. It is thought-provoking and informative. This book has much substance and is well organized." (California)

Never, Never Give Up

- "I am a 68-year-old businessman. At my age I should be enjoying a life way past retirement. It is not so. In 1997 Thailand suffered a severe economic crunch and my business almost went down under. It took me many years to try to come back. Just as I thought I was climbing out of the black hole, another crisis hit two years ago. This time I am too old to fight, but I have no choice but to go on. I thought that God and I were very close. However, after the first crisis hit I sort of lost my faith along with my hope. After the second crisis hit, I thought that God had forsaken me. I all but lost my faith totally until one day a good friend gave me a book, *Never, Never Give Up*. At first I didn't want to read it. However, insisted by my friend, I did. I stayed up the whole night finishing the book. By morning I kneeled down and begged God to forgive me for my foolishness. I felt so ashamed for my behavior. I begged Him to accept me back. After I did that, I know that God has forgiven me. Now I am back to feeling close to Him again. I am so happy and grateful for this book. God is great!" (Thailand)

- "Thanks for being there when you are so much needed by all of us. After seven major operations I am beginning to walk again and help others which is the full purpose of my existence which Jesus Christ has set before me. Your book, *Never, Never Give Up*, stayed by my pillow along with my Bible while I was recuperating from these operations. When I re-read it, I was charged with peace and energy again. The pain diminishes and I can speak of God's infinite love and mercy to others who are facing similar trials. Thank you for writing this God-inspired book." (Florida)

- "Suicide has shown its face in my mind. I found myself falling deeper and deeper into the pit of hell. My life seemed so grim. I could not see where I could make a difference and was planning to believe that if I chose to leave this life it would not matter. When I received *Never, Never Give Up* I read the first three chapters that evening. When I arrived at page ninety, your verse changed my life. I want you to know that I have been delivered from this season of trial. I rededicated my life to the Lord and feel wonderful. Thank you so much for your work. Through our Lord you have saved my life. Thank you for my life back." (Texas)

Overcoming Fear
- "Thank you for sending your books to the Philippines. I was very blessed to read *Overcoming Fear*. This book explained the sources of fear and what I should do to overcome fear. It is really a blessing to know all of this information that helped me to overcome the fear I have felt all these years. I have cherished every chapter in the book. It has become food for my soul. Thank you so much for explaining all of this so well. I have learned that I should never be afraid of anyone because I can be absolutely certain that God lives in my heart. This is great assurance because I know that God is greater than

anything I will ever face in this life. This book has been a great blessing in my life. God bless you both." (the Philippines)

- "I want to thank you immediately for your new book, *Overcoming Fear.* I have read every one of your books and given copies to many people, but I want to tell you that I believe this is your best book ever. I can hardly put it down. The day I received it I stayed up late, even though I was very tired, to read the first four chapters. The next morning I read two more chapters before going to work. This book is very inspiring. It gives me great peace. God's peace is so great that I cannot describe it. I have almost finished reading this book. When I am done, I will immediately read it again. Enclosed is a check for ten copies of this book plus a contribution to Lamplight Ministries. Thank you, Jack and Judy, for writing this wonderful book." (Massachusetts)

- "I want to thank you for publishing the book *Overcoming Fear.* I am reading mine for the second time. I cannot tell you how comforting it is. The way you have put information along with the right Bible verses is so truly helpful. As world conditions worsen, I can tell you that this book will be a constant companion alongside my Bible. I am so grateful for you both. Keep up the good work. You are making a big difference in peoples' lives. You have in mine." (Minnesota)

Victory Over Adversity

- "I am a pure and proud Dutchman married to a Tanzanian woman. I have had a lot of problems staying with an African wife in Europe. I love my wife so much, but the environment for my wife was not good enough in terms of getting a job. This affected us very much to the extent that I was even planning to relocate to Tanzania for the sake of my wife and children's future. Thank God that an angel was sent to me by the name of Jim who gave me a book, *Victory over Adversity.* This book is amazing and great. It contains the answers to my problems and is a great encouragement to me. As a Dutchman I find it very interesting to read a book with simple English. Putting the facts of this book into practice has changed my life greatly. I have found a new job. My wife has found a good job. The thoughts of relocating to Tanzania have faded. My faith has increased and my commitment to God has grown. I pray that God will bless the writers of this book and also the man who gave me this book. My wife and I are always reading this book. It is our source of strength." (Holland)

- "I praise God for His living Word. Thank you for the books that you have sent to China. You cannot imagine what *Victory over Adversity* did in my life as a young believer. Not only is the language clear and accessible, but the content is very rewarding. I learned a lot from this book. I now meditate day and night on the Word of God. I am in the presence of God often. I am confident that I can overcome any adversity in the precious name of Jesus Christ. May God bless you and fill you with His infinite grace, Mr. Jack and his wife." (China)

- "I am a 22-year-old college student in Thailand. My family is half Christian. My mother is a Christian whereas my father is a Buddhist. I am the eldest daughter of my parents with one younger brother and sister. All three of us have been baptized as Christians since birth. Frankly, I have never had much faith in God and always have had problems with both of my parents. I think that they don't understand me. They think I don't listen to them. Last month my mother was given a book, *Victory over Adversity,* by her friend. Out of curiosity I took the book and read it before she did. I could not put it down. For the first time I felt that God is real and is close to me. I cried and cried and felt sorry for my past behavior toward God and my parents. I went to my mother and apologized, to her great surprise. Now I go to church with her every Sunday. I am very thankful to my mother's friend who gave her this book and also to the writers of this book who have changed my life and brought me to God which my mother could not do. Thank you both!" (Thailand)

Exchange Your Worries for God's Perfect Peace
- "*Exchange Your Worries for God's Perfect Peace* is a masterpiece. I am reading this book to the people here in the

Philippines. I saw tears flowing down their faces as I read them parts of this book. I must get this book translated into their language. I am reading this book for the second time. After 30 years in the ministry I have finally learned how to turn my worries over to God. I have learned more from this book in the last few months than I have ever learned in my life. I will not allow my copy of this book to leave my presence. I thank God for you." (the Philippines)

- "I just want to tell you how much I appreciate you and your excellent book, *Exchange Your Worries for God's Perfect Peace*. I have read all of your books several times each. I continually go back to refer to the notes I have made in your books. I have done this for close to 15 years and pages are falling out of your books. I read the Bible daily. Your books are a close second to the Bible. I have never found another Christian author who teaches me more about God's Word and speaks directly to my heart as your writings do. Thank you for helping me appreciate and respect the Word of God." (Wisconsin)

- "I was in despair struggling with my life and ministry. *Exchange Your Worries for God's Perfect Peace* has strengthened me and encouraged my heart. My country is often threatened by disasters. Your book and the Scripture in it has helped me to focus on God, no matter what circumstances I have experienced and will face in the future. The language in the book is very clear and easy to understand for someone like me who uses English as a second language. I have been blessed by reading this book. My faith in Jesus has increased. Thank you for sending this book to me. I thank God that I know you. You are a blessing." (Indonesia)

God's Joy Regardless of Circumstances
- "*God's Joy Regardless of Circumstances* came to me right on time. Being in prison for 20 years for a crime I didn't commit and then having to deal with severe family problems is not a morsel that is easy to swallow. My oldest daughter was

pregnant and we were looking forward to having my first grandson born. We were very pained to learn that my daughter had to lose her baby. In the midst of dealing with this problem, you sent me a free copy of *God's Joy Regardless of Circumstances.* When I avidly started to read this book, my daughter underwent surgery, lost her baby and faced uncertainty and despair. *God's Joy Regardless of Circumstances* pulled us through. Thank you also for sending a free copy of this book to my daughter. May God continue blessing Lamplight Ministries." (Florida)

- "Many thanks for sending me *God's Joy Regardless of Circumstances*. This book has been a real stream in the desert that I have been able to drink from. I have been blessed tremendously by this book. My life has not been the same since I started reading it. I have used this book to help many people on my radio programme every Sunday. Many people have given their lives to Christ because of these messages." (Zambia)

- "Only this year I faced a lot of challenges. As a result I became bitter at heart. The wonderful Scripture verses in *God's Joy Regardless of Circumstances* took away my bitterness. I am happy now. This book has instructed me how to handle any situation with God's joy. I now can see God's solution to my life challenges by the presence of God's joy inside me. Your God-given insight has given new meaning to my spiritual life. Thank you for the encouragement through your writings." (Lome-Togo West Africa)

God's Instructions for Growing Older
- "*God's Instructions for Growing Older* is the very best and most comprehensive book we have ever found on this subject. We absolutely love the way that Jack and Judy continually build on the knowledge from the previous chapters, always reminding what was learned before, and then adding another layer of knowledge to that. We would suggest *God's Instructions for Growing Older* as a must have manual for every person we know. Well done, Jack and Judy! (Wisconsin)

- "I have never read a book like *God's Instructions for Growing Older*. Finally a book has been written that teaches how to finish our course in life as a Christian. Your chapter on Scripture meditation is pure gold. This book is a road map to direct us in the way the Lord intends for us to grow older. Thank you so much for this special book." (Florida)

- "Thank you for your new book, *God's Instructions for Growing Older*. I love this book. I read a little bit every day so that I can be an encourager to my older friends and to myself. We so need God's knowledge during the final years of our lives. I have started my gift list to share this book with others." (Texas)

God's Wisdom Is Available to You

- "I did not sleep last night after reading your book *God's Wisdom is Available to You*. Thank you for your wonderful work. Because of persecution against my ministry, I spent a considerable amount of time in the hospital because of depression. I am now well and healthy in Jesus' name. Thank you for your help. I will be teaching members of my church from key text in your book. Please be my mentor, teacher and counselor." (Ghana)

- I thank God each and every day for Jack and Judy Hartman. When I started reading your book on wisdom, everything was going wrong in my life. This book revived my spirit and my faith in God. It has changed my life. The Bible used to be like Greek to me. Now I can read it and understand it. I can't put this book down because I know I need to absorb it. I'm going through it for a second time. This book is one of the best things that has ever happened to me. I thank you both and I thank God." (Florida)

- "You did a fantastic job on this book. It is an encyclopedia on God's wisdom. The writing style is just great. Many books don't bring the reader through the subject the way this book does. I'm very impressed with that. You have made it a real joy for me to study and re-digest Scripture. This book has been very good for me." (North Carolina)

A Close and Intimate Relationship with God
- "Your book, *A Close and Intimate Relationship with God,* is tremendous. I thought that I had a close relationship with God, but this book really opened my eyes. I now can see many things that I still need to do to be even closer to God. I couldn't put this book down. When I had to stop reading, I couldn't wait to get back to it the next day. Every chapter is filled with Scripture that is very helpful to me. I will be making many changes in my life as a result of reading this awesome book. Thank you and God bless you." (New Hampshire)

- "Thank you for giving me a copy of your book *A Close and Intimate Relationship with God.* This book is written so clearly that all instructions are to the point. My life has been greatly changed and refreshed. The presence of God has become very strong in my life. I am at peace trusting my God to meet every need. My mind is totally on God. I can clearly hear His voice. I am receiving guidance and direction from Him as a result of this book. I cannot afford to spend a day without reading this book. I carry it with me wherever I go." (Zambia)

- "Thank you for your book titled *A Close and Intimate Relationship with God.* This inspiring book helped me to draw closer to our heavenly Father. In Chapter 25 you said that Paul and Silas were praising God in prison. I was having a challenging day when I read this chapter. God spoke through your book to praise Him no matter what circumstances I faced. Thank you for that inspiration. The information on dying to self in the last chapter where Paul said that he dies daily really encouraged me. I am learning to do much better putting God first, others second and myself last. Thank you at Lamplight Ministries for the thousands of people around the world that you are supporting. May the dear Lord bless you abundantly." (China)

Unshakable Faith in Almighty God
- "I thank God for the book *Unshakable Faith in Almighty God.* Because I am not indigenous Chinese, it is not easy to

fellowship with the local Chinese. When I got this book I was able to see a way in the wilderness. It became my guide and light every day. When I was just about to give up Christianity, God at the right time provided this book to me. The truths and clear instruction in this book are direct from the throne of God. I am determined to move on with God come what may. I praise God that is He able to raise people we have never seen like Jack and Judy Hartman to speak into our lives through their publications. God bless the Hartman family. One day when Christ comes it will be exciting for them to see how they have influenced the world for God in Jesus' name. I am so grateful for these free books that cost a lot of money in publishing, printing and postage." (China)

- "I have been pastoring in Belgium for the past 15 years. In the past our church was flourishing and doing very well until late last year when my praise and worship leader decided to break away and form another church. This was a very big blow to us as a church. Most of our strong and committed members left the church with some of the church instruments. My wife almost gave up. She was discouraged. This also affected our finances. Pastor Jim gave me a book titled *Unshakable Faith in Almighty God*. Before I read this book my faith was shaken and I almost gave up. This book took me step by step to show me how to make my faith grow. You cannot read this book and remain the same. I have been using the book to preach to the few members that remain with us. In the past four months we have experienced revival. The anointing is so strong and the members have been strengthened so much through the preaching from this book. We are determined to not give up. God bless the Hartmans for being a blessing to us in Europe." (Belgium)

- "*Unshakable Faith in Almighty God* has amazed me. The language is so simple and very clear to understand. This book is powerful and life-changing. I will always hang on to this book. Brother Hartman, God's favour and wisdom are so great on your life. I believe this book is written on very heavy anointing from God. Your reward in heaven will be so great. All those who have sown seeds in your ministry should rejoice. When I wake up, I read this book. Before going to bed, I read it. I will continue to go through it again and again. Your ministry is a big blessing to me. You are always in our prayers." (Zambia)

How to Study the Bible

- "Your book, *How to Study the Bible*, is a gem. Since I became a Christian 41 years ago, I have studied the Bible using a variety of methods. Your method is simple and straightforward. It involves hard work, but the rewards are real. I have read several of your books and this book is the one I would highly recommend to any Christian because this book is the foundation. God bless you, brother." (England)

- "My wife and I are utilizing the Bible study method that you explained in *How to Study the Bible*. We are really growing spiritually as a result. Our old methods of study were not nearly as fruitful. Thank you for writing about your method." (Idaho)

- "I have read almost all of your books and they are outstanding. The one that blessed me the most was *How to Study the Bible*. The study part was excellent, but the meditation chapters were very, very beneficial. I am indebted to you for sharing these. I purchased 30 copies to give to friends. Every earnest student of God's Word needs a copy." (Tennessee)

Increased Energy and Vitality

- "It is so great to meet Christians on the same wave length. In your book *Increased Energy and Vitality*, you are writing almost word for word in some cases what I have been saying to patients for almost 30 years." (Ohio)

- "Last year I obtained a copy of your book *Increased Energy and Vitality*. My wife and I have read and have in fact changed our ways of eating and drinking and exercising because of your influence. We thoroughly appreciate this God-centered message that is so well presented. I have enclosed an order for more of these books. We know many people we wish to help. This is the first step in spreading the news you have so generously put together. Thank you for your efforts. May God continue your leadership in writing, speaking and guidance." (Illinois)

- "I have benefited tremendously from reading and personally applying the principles learned from your book *Increased Energy and Vitality*. By applying your methods, I have gained additional energy especially during my low periods from 2:00 p.m. to 4:00 p.m. I highly recommend your book to others. Keep up the good work." (Florida)

100 Years from Today

- "*100 Years From Today* told me that going to church and doing good deeds won't get me to heaven. I believe in Jesus Christ. I believe He died for our sins and that He forgives us for what we did wrong. Heaven is where I belong. I am born again. I have a new life. This book has changed my life." (Florida)

- "I am writing to express my deep and profound appreciation for your book *100 Years from Today*. I recently began attending a Bible-based church where I found a copy of this book in their lending library. I read the book in one sitting, reading the words aloud to myself. Your book explained details from the Bible that I had not learned before. I thank you for taking the time and effort to write this book. My written words can never fully express how grateful I am to you. By my actions, a changed life and a deep sense of peace, I hope to bear fruit by helping others." (Massachusetts)

- "I find it hard to put *100 Years from Today* down. I read the whole book in a day and a half. I never knew how much pain and suffering Jesus went through to pay for my sins. I learned how much He loves us." (Florida)

Nuggets of Faith

- "Your books, tapes and meditation cards are really a blessing to me. They came at just the right time. I am preparing sermons on faith from *Nuggets of Faith*. I want the congregation to be constantly learning God's Word in order to have much more faith. I also have been encouraged personally through that book. It is awesome. Thank you for your powerful and inspiring publications." (Zambia)

- "We give *Nuggets of Faith* to people who are hospitalized, for birthdays, to saved and unsaved. Everyone who has received one tells us 'It's the best little book I've ever read. It's so clear and easy to understand.'" (Indiana)

- "I work as a store manager. Today I was told that I was no longer needed. Praise Jesus that only two months prior to this date I had accepted the Lord Jesus as my personal Lord and Savior. I have faith that the Lord was working to bring me to a new direction. I am writing to thank you for your excellent book *Nuggets of Faith*. The moment I arrived home after having been dismissed, I received this book in the mail. I completed this short but awesome book in a little over two hours. It has helped my faith to grow stronger and I know that I will begin a great new journey tomorrow. God bless you." (New York)

COMMENTS ON OUR SCRIPTURE MEDITATION CARDS

- "My back was hurting so badly that I couldn't get comfortable. I was miserable whether I sat or stood or laid down. I didn't know what to do. Suddenly I thought of the Scripture cards on healing that my husband had purchased. I decided to meditate on the Scripture in these cards. I was only on the second card when, all of a sudden, I felt heat go from my neck down through my body. The Lord had healed me. I never knew it could happen so fast. The pain has not come back." (Idaho)

- "My wife and I use your Scripture cards every day when we pray. I read the card for that day in English and then my wife repeats it in Norwegian. We then pray based upon the Scripture reference on that day's card. These cards have been very beneficial to us. We would like to see the Scripture cards published in the Norwegian language." (Norway)

- "Your Scripture cards have been very helpful to my wife and myself. We have taped them to the walls in our home and we meditate on them constantly. I also take four or five cards with me every day when I go to work. I meditate on them while I drive. The Scripture on these cards is a constant source of encouragement to us. We ask for permission to translate *Trust God for Your Finances*. This book is badly needed by the people in Turkey." (This permission was granted.) (Turkey)

- "My mom is 95 years old. She was in the Bergen-Belsen Concentration Camp in Germany from 1943 to 1945. She has always had a lot of worry and fear. My mother was helped greatly in overcoming this problem by your Scripture cards titled *Freedom from Worry and Fear*. She was helped so much that she asked me to order another set to give to a friend." (California)

- "I am overwhelmed about the revelations in your Scripture Meditation Cards. These Scripture cards have helped me so much that I cannot write enough on this sheet of paper. We have gone through a five-day programme in our church using the Scripture cards. My faith has increased tremendously. I no longer am submitting to my own will and desires, but I am now submitting to the will of God and it is so fantastic. God bless you, Jack and Judy Hartman." (Ghana)

- "I am very enthusiastic about your Scripture cards and your tape titled *Receive Healing from the Lord*. I love your tape. The clarity of your voice and your sincerity and compassion will encourage sick people. They can listen to this tape throughout the day, before they go to sleep at night, while they are driving to the doctor's office, in the hospital, etc. The tape is filled with Scripture and many good comments on Scripture. This cassette tape and your Scripture cards on healing are powerful tools that will help many sick people." (Tennessee) (NOTE: The ten cassette tapes for our Scripture Meditation Cards are available on 60 minute CDs as well.)

- "I meditate constantly on the healing cards and listen to your tape on healing over and over. Your voice is so soothing. You are a wonderful teacher. My faith is increasing constantly." (New Hampshire).

- "I thank God for you. I carry your Scripture Meditation Cards in my purse. The Scriptures you have chosen are all powerful. What a blessing to be able to meditate on the Word of God at any time, anywhere. Thank you for your hard work. The Scripture cards are a blessing to me." (Canada)

Books written by Jack Hartman
Trust God for Your Finances
What Will Heaven Be Like?
Never, Never Give Up
How to Study the Bible
Quiet Confidence in the Lord
One Hundred Years from Today
Nuggets of Faith
God's Will for Your Life

Books co-authored by Jack and Judy Hartman
You Can Hear the Voice of God
God's Instructions for Growing Older
Effective Prayer
Overcoming Fear
A Close and Intimate Relationship with God
God's Joy Regardless of Circumstances
Victory Over Adversity
What Does God Say?
Receive Healing from the Lord
Unshakable Faith in Almighty God
Exchange Your Worries for God's Perfect Peace
God's Wisdom Is Available to You
Increased Energy and Vitality

**Scripture Meditation Cards
co-authored by Jack and Judy Hartman**
Receive Healing from the Lord
Freedom from Worry and Fear
Enjoy God's Wonderful Peace
God Is Always with You
Continually Increasing Faith in God
Receive God's Blessings in Adversity
Financial Instructions from God
Find God's Will for Your Life
A Closer Relationship with the Lord
Our Father's Wonderful Love

You Can Hear the Voice of God

Jack and Judy Hartman

Lamplight Ministries, Inc.
Dunedin, Florida

We are so pleased that you have chosen to read this book. We believe that you will do much more than read *You Can Hear the Voice of God*. We believe that you will hear God's voice as a result of reading through this book. We can't wait for you to tell us what has happened. Please visit our website at www.lamplight.net and tell us about your adventure or call 1-800-540-1597 (ask for Judy) or drop us a note in the mail.

You also can call 1-800-540-1597 to request our free newsletter by mail or email. We would be so pleased to stay in touch with you with our newsletter. You can see updates on our next books and keep us in prayer as we pray for you. You also can receive a daily Devotional that is one of our Scripture meditation cards. You can download the first chapter of each of our books. We are blessed that you will get to know us through the pages of this book. We will look forward to hearing from you. We look forward to getting to know you.

Copyright 2012

Jack and Judy Hartman

No part of this book may be used or reproduced in any manner whatsoever without written permission from the publisher except in the case of brief quotations and articles of review. For more information regarding this book please contact:

Jack and Judy Hartman
Lamplight Ministries Inc.
PO Box 1307
Dunedin, Florida 34697-2921

Telephone: 1-800-540-1597
FAX: 1-727-784-2980
Website: www.lamplight.net
Email: jackandjudy@lamplight.net

ISBN: 978-0915445-24-0

Library of Congress Control Number: 2012916693

Dedication

We dedicate this book to Drs. Rodney and Adonica Howard-Browne. We had the privilege of attending the River Church for three years until they moved to their new location. Jack had the high honor of teaching in the River Bible Institute during its first year of existence. Judy attended the River Bible Institute for one semester in its first year. All outreaches of The River are about experiencing God and sharing that experience with others.

Pastors Rodney and Adonica are so full of Jesus Christ. You cannot be near them or attend a service without coming closer to the Lord. They remind us of Paul who said, "It is okay to do as I do. I am doing my best to follow Jesus. I will direct you to Jesus Christ." (Judy's paraphrase).

God has anointed this precious couple from South Africa to reach America with the love of God through Jesus Christ. They have done outreaches in many countries, but their focus right now is in touching the United States of America with the gospel of Jesus Christ. We enthusiastically invite you to www.revival.com.

The River is not about expanding itself, but it is about equipping the saints to share the gospel. We urge you to go to the River to be trained in evangelism. You will never be the same.

Pastors Rodney and Adonica, we thank God that you heard His voice and left your homeland to come to America with only $300 in your pockets. We thank God that you have continued to listen to His voice as He has directed you to a vision that, as you have always taught, must be bigger than you could ever do by yourselves. We thank you for hearing the voice of God and obeying Him and for igniting people in America and across the world to do the same.

We pray God's continued blessing on you, on your dear family and on the vision that God has given you. We love you.

Jack and Judy

We each began studying the Bible in the *King James Version*. If we could write this entire book with the *King James Version*, we would. However, we want to present the reader with the best possible explanation of each verse of Scripture.

We have reviewed each verse of Scripture in this book to prayerfully select the Bible version that we believe will help you to best understand what God is saying to you. In some cases we have used *The New International Version* (NIV) when we believe the language in this particular passage of Scripture will give you more comprehension. In other cases we have used *The Amplified Bible* (AMP) when we believe the amplification will explain more to you.

The *King James Version* (KJV) of the Bible received its name from King James who was the king of England from 1603 to 1625. King James is considered to have been one of the most intellectual and learned kings in the history of Great Britain. He is primarily remembered for authorizing the production of the *King James Version* of the Bible. This English translation from Greek and Hebrew is the most printed book in the history of the world with more than one billion copies in print.

The New International Version (NIV) is the result of the study of a group of approximately 100 Hebrew and Greek scholars representing more than 20 denominations. This team of scholars devoted 10 years to complete the NIV translation. The goal of this committee was to faithfully translate the original Greek, Hebrew and Aramaic biblical text into clearly understandable English. The NIV is the most widely purchased contemporary Bible today.

The Amplified Bible is the result of the study of a group of Bible scholars who spent a total of more than 20,000 hours amplifying the Bible. They believe that traditional word-by-word translation often fails to reveal the shades of meaning that are part of the original Greek, Hebrew and Aramaic biblical texts.

Any amplification of the original text uses brackets for words that clarify the meaning and parentheses for words that contain additional phrases included in the original language. Through this amplification the reader will gain a better understanding of what Hebrew and Greek listeners instinctively understood.

Scripture quotations marked (KJV) are taken from the *King James Version* of the Bible.

Scripture quotations marked (NIV) are taken from *The Holy Bible, New International Version,* copyright 1973, 1978, 1984 by International Bible Society. Used by permission of Zondervan Publishing House.

Scripture quotations marked (AMP) are taken from *The Amplified Bible*, Old Testament, copyright 1965, 1987 by the Zondervan Corporation, Grand Rapids Michigan, or *The Amplified Bible*, New Testament, copyright 1954, 1958, 1987 by the Lockman Foundation, LaHabra, California. Used by permission.

TABLE OF CONTENTS

Introduction	31
1. God Knows Every Minute Detail about You	35
2. You Are Able to Hear God Speaking to You	39
3. Learn How to Hear God's Voice	43
4. God Will Teach You and Encourage You	47
5. God Will Guide You Continually	51
6. Expect to Hear God Speaking to You	55
7. Intimacy with God and Hearing God's Voice	61
8. Program Yourself to Hear God's Voice	67
9. Are You in Awe of the Word of God?	73
10. Obey God's Instructions	81
11. Turn Away from the Ways of the World	87
12. The Importance of Daily Quiet Time with God	93
13. You Hear the Voice of God within Yourself	99
14. The Voice of God and the Voice of Satan	103
15. Do Not Block Yourself from Hearing God's Voice	111
16. Humble Yourself and Keep God in First Place	117
17. Fear God and Focus on Him	121
18. Praise God and Thank Him Continually	125
19. Be Calm, Quiet and Confident within Yourself	125
20. Final Thoughts on Hearing the Voice of God	137
Conclusion	143
Appendix	145
Study Guide	151

Introduction

We will begin this book by looking into the first chapter of the first book in the Bible. The words "God said" are used nine times in this chapter. God *spoke* the world and everything in the world into existence. In this book we will explain that the same God Who created everything on earth by speaking speaks to *you* throughout every day of your life.

This statement may seem incredulous to you, but we will show you from the Word of God that God actually is able to speak to every one of the billions of people in the world at the same time. God wants you to learn how to hear what He is saying to you.

Unbelievers are unable to hear God's voice. In this book we will study Scripture that will explain that, if Jesus Christ is your Savior, you have been given the opportunity to hear God's voice (If you are not certain that Jesus Christ is your Savior, please stop reading now and turn to the Appendix at the end of this book). Once you see for yourself that you can hear God speaking, you then will be ready to learn how to hear God's voice.

Many Christians do not hear God speaking to them because they do not know what the Word of God says about hearing God's voice. You do not need to search your Bible for specific instructions that tell you how to hear God's voice. We have done this work for you. We pray that you will take full advantage of the hundreds of hours we have spent finding these verses of Scripture, arranging them in an orderly sequence and explaining them to you.

This book is not filled with theological language that is difficult to understand. All Scripture references that we use are accompanied by a simple and easy-to-understand explanation. Our goal is to simplify God's instructions on hearing His voice.

As you study these Scripture references, you will understand the vital importance of learning how to hear God's voice. *You decide* how frequently you will hear God's voice. If you learn and obey the specific instructions that God has given to you, you will be able to hear God speaking to you continually.

We explained just before the Table of Contents that we use three versions of the Bible in our books – *The King James Version, The New International Version* and *The Amplified Bible*. We use *The Amplified Bible* much more than the other versions. The reason for this is that you are given, on the average, approximately *35% more information* on each passage of Scripture through the amplification.

I (Jack) have been using *The Amplified Bible* since 1975. At that time only *The Amplified New Testament* was available. I bought this version of the Bible when I saw it in a bookstore with an inscription on the cover from Dr. Billy Graham saying, "This is the best Study Testament on the market. It is a magnificent translation. I use it constantly."

We would like to give you an example as to why we use *The Amplified Bible* more than any other version:

- "I can do all things through Christ which strengtheneth me." (Philippians 4:13 KJV)
- "I can do all this through him who gives me strength." (Philippians 4:13 NIV)
- "I have strength for all things in Christ Who empowers me [I am ready for anything and equal to anything through Him Who infuses inner strength into me; I am self-sufficient in Christ's sufficiency]." (Philippians 4:13 AMP)

Please note the tremendous amplification of the original Greek in *The Amplified Bible.* If you want to meditate on one of these three versions of Philippians 4:13, you will find that there is much more to meditate on in *The Amplified Bible* version. We have found that Scripture references in *The Amplified Bible* often contain a great deal of additional information that is not found in other versions of the Bible.

As you read this book, we recommend that you highlight or underline all passages of Scripture and our explanation that are helpful to you. Write notes in the margin. If you do, you then will be able to go back through this book after you have read it the first time. You will be able to carefully study and meditate on important passages of Scripture that you already have identified.

I (Jack) want to explain why I often use the first person on many occasions in our books. I write the first two drafts of each book. Judy then adds her valuable input to the next two drafts. I then write the final two drafts.

I do not want to use the words "I (Jack)" every time that I use a first-person reference. I will just use the word "I" when I make a personal observation. Any personal observations from Judy will be clearly identified.

We pray that the scriptural contents of this book and our explanation of this Scripture will stir up a deep hunger within you to hear God speaking to you every day of your life. We pray that your life will be transformed as you learn and apply God's instructions for hearing His voice.

Chapter 1

God Knows Every Minute Detail about You

Both the Old Testament and New Testament contain many stories of God speaking to people. God talked to Abraham, Moses, David, Noah and many other people. God did not speak only to these leaders. The Bible contains other stories of God speaking to people who were not leaders. God is the same now as He was then. He has not stopped speaking to people. "…I am the Lord, I do not change…" (Malachi 3:6 AMP)

If God spoke to these people, you can be certain that He will speak to you today. "…God shows no partiality and is no respecter of persons" (Acts 10:34 AMP)

Some people believe that God is too busy dealing with important matters to be able to talk to them. They do not understand that God is omnipresent. He is able to talk to billions of people throughout the world at the same time. "One God and Father of [us] all, Who is above all [Sovereign over all], pervading all and [living] in [us] all." (Ephesians 4:6 AMP)

This verse of Scripture explains that God is the Father of every person who has received Jesus Christ as his or her Savior. God is seated on His throne in heaven where He is above all and sovereign over all. You also are told that God pervades all. The word "pervade" means to be spread out. God can be in an infinite number of places at the same time. In addition to being in heaven, God is spread out all over the world. He lives in the heart of every person who has received Jesus Christ as his or her Savior.

Latest estimates state that the population of the world is slightly over seven billion people. Because God is omnipresent, He can talk to billions of people at the same time. Do not attempt to bring God down to the limitations of your human understanding. God is fully able to communicate with every person in the world in whatever language or dialect they speak. "Who among the gods is like you, Lord? Who is like you – majestic in holiness, awesome in glory, working wonders?" (Exodus 15:11 NIV)

God is mighty, awesome and majestic. Nothing is too difficult for Him. "Alas, Lord God! Behold, You have made the heavens and the earth by Your great power and by Your outstretched arm! There is nothing too hard or too wonderful for You" (Jeremiah 32:17 AMP)

The same God Who created heaven and earth and every person on earth is ready, willing and able to speak continually to *you*. "…He Who forms the mountains and creates the wind and declares to man what is his thought…" (Amos 4:13 AMP)

The same God Who creates mountains and causes the wind to blow knows exactly what you are thinking. God knows every minute detail about you. The psalmist David said "O Lord, you have searched me [thoroughly] and have known me. You know my downsitting and my uprising; You understand my thought afar off. You sift and search out my path and my lying down, and You are acquainted with all my ways. For there is not a word in my tongue [still unuttered], but, behold, O Lord, You know it altogether." (Psalm 139:1-4 AMP)

David understood that God knew when he sat down and when he stood up. David knew that God understood exactly what he was thinking and that He knew every word he was about to say before he spoke. "…not a creature exists that is concealed from His sight, but all things are open and exposed, naked and defenseless to the eyes of Him with Whom we have to do." (Hebrews 4:13 AMP)

This verse explains that God knows *everything* about every person on earth. You can be certain that the same Almighty God Who created you knows about every minute detail of your life. God is fully able to speak to you many times each day to give you specific personal advice that you require in your life.

God actually knows every hair on the head of every one of the billions of people on earth (see Matthew 10:30). God loves you with incredible unconditional love. If Jesus Christ is your Savior, God is speaking to you today to guide you, help you and to teach you whatever you need to know. Do not block yourself from hearing God's voice by thinking that He is too busy to speak to you or that He does not care about what is important to you.

You are a unique person. The fingerprints of every person on earth are different from the fingerprints of every other person. Every person has a different DNA. Your Father will say things to you throughout every day of your life that He does not say to anyone else. He has unique individual messages for each and every one of His beloved children.

The psalmist was in awe that the God of the universe actually desires a close and intimate relationship with every person on earth. He said, "When I view and consider Your heavens, the work of Your fingers, the moon and the stars, which You have ordained and established, what is man that You are mindful of him, and the son of [earthborn] man that You care for him?" (Psalm 8:3-4 AMP)

The psalmist wondered why God Who created heaven and earth, the moon, the stars and every other planet and galaxy also cares about the intimate details of the lives of billions of human beings. As we study more and more Scripture in this book, you will see that God really does speak to *you* continually. God knows all about your faults and shortcomings. He loves you unconditionally regardless of any shortcomings that you may have.

Do not block yourself from hearing God speaking because you think you are not worthy of hearing His voice. This belief is correct. *No one* is worthy of hearing God's voice. However, if Jesus Christ is your Savior, Jesus has paid the full price to enable you to hear God speaking to you.

In this first chapter we have established a foundation to show you that the same God Who spoke to people in the Bible speaks to you today. We have explained that God is omnipresent. He lives in your heart if Jesus Christ is your Savior. He is with you throughout every day of your life.

The same God Who spoke to people in the Bible is speaking to you today. There is no question that God is speaking to you. *Will you* learn how to hear His voice?

In subsequent chapters we will explain in more detail that God does speak to people continually. We will devote the remainder of this book to show you exactly what God instructs you to do so that you will be able to hear what He is saying to you.

Chapter 2

You Are Able to Hear God Speaking to You

In the last chapter you learned many important scriptural truths about God's supernatural ability to speak at the same time to every person in the world. In this chapter we will look into the holy Scriptures for more specific information pertaining to God's desire to speak continually to you. We will explain the importance of you learning how to consistently hear His voice.

Unbelievers cannot hear God's voice. Their sins have blocked them from being able to hear God's voice. "…your iniquities have made a separation between you and your God, and your sins have hidden His face from you..." (Isaiah 59:2 AMP)

The sins of unbelievers are a spiritual barrier that separates them from God. If you receive Jesus Christ as your Savior, the barrier that blocked you from hearing God's voice is taken away. "…if any person is [ingrafted] in Christ (the Messiah) he is a new creation (a new creature altogether); the old [previous moral and spiritual condition] has passed away. Behold, the fresh and new has come!" (II Corinthians 5:17 AMP)

The word "ingrafted" in the amplification of this verse means to become one with. When you receive Jesus Christ as your Savior, you become one with Him. The enormous price that Jesus paid at Calvary has cleansed you from all sin. You become a brand new person in the spiritual realm. You now are able to hear the voice of God.

All sins that you have committed in the past have disappeared from the consciousness of God. Your loving Father has *forgotten* every sin that you have ever committed, no matter how severe this sin might have been. God said, "For I will be merciful and gracious toward their sins and I will remember their deeds of unrighteousness no more." (Hebrews 8:12 AMP)

From God's perspective you are just as clean before Him as Jesus is. God looks at you as if you had never sinned. If Jesus Christ is your Savior, there is absolutely no question that you have been given the ability to hear the voice of God. "Whoever is of God listens to God. [Those who belong to God hear the words of God.]…" (John 8:47 AMP)

If Jesus is your Savior, you belong to God. You can hear exactly what He is saying to you. Jesus said, "…To you it has been given to know the secrets and mysteries of the kingdom of heaven, but to them it has not been given." (Matthew 13:11 AMP)

You receive many wonderful blessings when you receive Jesus Christ as your Savior. Jesus explained that you will "know the secrets and mysteries of the kingdom heaven" if He is your Savior. You will know great spiritual truths that unbelievers have no way of knowing.

If Jesus is your Savior, God is speaking to you many times throughout every day of your life. God "…speaks not only once, but more than once, even though men do not regard it…" (Job 33:14 AMP)

God's words fall on deaf ears in the lives of many Christians because they do not understand that God is speaking to them. These Christians do not know how to hear what God is saying. God said, "Behold, I stand at the door and knock; if anyone hears and listens to and heeds My voice and opens the door, I will come in to him and will eat with him, and he [will eat] with Me." (Revelation 3:20 AMP)

God wants you to hear what He is saying to you. You will hear His voice if you learn what His Word instructs you to do to hear what He is saying to you. Jesus said, "He who has ears to hear, let him be listening and let him consider and perceive and comprehend by hearing." (Matthew 11:15 AMP)

If Jesus Christ is your Savior, you *do* have ears to hear. There is so much that God wants to say to you if you will learn how to hear His voice.

God often emphasizes through repetition. Jesus repeated the same words shortly after the statement He made in Matthew 11:15. Jesus said, "He who has ears [to hear], let him be listening and let him consider and perceive and comprehend by hearing." (Matthew 13:9 AMP)

Jesus has emphasized through repetition so that you will listen to God and learn from Him. Do not be one of the many Christians who have been given the ability to hear God's voice but never hear what God is saying.

Many Christians make a major mistake because they do not take advantage of the magnificent opportunity that they have been given to hear God speaking to them. Jesus said, "…Be careful what you are hearing. The measure [of thought and study] you give [to the truth you hear] will be the measure [of virtue and knowledge] that comes back to you – and more [besides] will be given to you who hear." (Mark 4:24 AMP)

When Jesus spoke of being careful about what you are hearing, He referred to consistently hearing the Word of God instead of constantly listening to things in the world. If you do, you will receive magnificent spiritual knowledge, understanding and comprehension. The more you learn, the more you will be able to learn. Do not make the mistake of consistently listening to the things of the world and blocking out the great things that God wants to say to you.

When you receive Jesus Christ as your Savior, you receive the spiritual eyes and spiritual ears of the hidden person of the heart who lives inside of you (see I Peter 3:4). When you read the Bible, you are able to understand what God is saying to you even though you could not understand the holy Scriptures before you were saved. You can understand because of the spiritual discernment that you were given when Jesus became your Savior.

If you have been a Christian very long and you have consistently studied the Word of God, you know that what we are saying is true. You know that you are able to understand what God is saying in His Word when you could not understand the Bible before you were saved. This same principle applies to your spiritual ears. You have been given the ability to hear God's voice. Make learning how to hear God's voice a top priority in your life.

God gave you a precious gift when He gave you the ability to hear His voice. You did not earn this gift. You do not deserve this gift. This gift has been given to you by the grace of God, the love of God and the enormous price that Jesus Christ paid for you when He shed His precious blood for you and took your sins upon Himself.

You will not hear God's voice automatically because you are saved. You must learn *how* to hear what God is saying to you. This book is filled with Scripture that will explain exactly what you should do so that you will be able to hear God speaking to you throughout every day and night of your life.

Chapter 3

Learn How to Hear God's Voice

In this chapter you will learn from God's Word that, if Jesus Christ is your Savior, God is your loving Father. You are His beloved child. You will learn that God wants you to hear His voice and how much your life will be changed if you learn how to consistently hear what your Father is saying to you. God said, "…I will be a Father to you, and you shall be My sons and daughters, says the Lord Almighty." (II Corinthians 6:18 AMP)

Jesus paid an awesome price so that you can be a member of the family of God. "…you are no longer outsiders (exiles, migrants, and aliens, excluded from the rights of citizens), but you now share citizenship with the saints (God's own people, consecrated and set apart for Himself); and you belong to God's [own] household." (Ephesians 2:19 AMP)

Please note the words "you belong to God's own household" in this verse and the amplification. You are not an outsider any more. God loves you so much that He has made it possible for *you* to be His beloved child. "See what [an incredible] quality of love the Father has given (shown, bestowed on) us, that we should [be permitted to] be named and called and counted the children of God! And so we are!..." (I John 3:1 AMP)

Whenever you think of God, think of Him as your loving Father. "…to all who did receive him, to those who believed in his name, he gave the right to become children of God – children born not of natural descent, nor of human decision or a husband's will, but born of God." (John 1:12-13 NIV)

You were born into the family of God, not through natural birth as you were born to your earthly parents, but as a result of the tremendous sacrifice that Jesus made for you. God loves you so much that He has made it possible for you, with all of your faults and shortcomings, to actually become a member of His royal family. Jesus paid the full price to cleanse you from *every* sin that you have ever committed. All Christians are "…blameless and guileless, innocent and uncontaminated, children of God without blemish (faultless, unrebukable)…" (Philippians 2:15 AMP)

God looks at *you* as "blameless, faultless and without blemish." You saw in the last chapter that God has forgotten all of your past sins (see Hebrews 8:12). He does not want you to remember them. You are His cleansed and innocent child. "…in Christ Jesus you are all children of God through faith." (Galatians 3:26 NIV)

Please note the word "all" in this verse of Scripture. Every person who has received Jesus Christ as his or her Savior is a son or daughter of God. You can be certain that *you really are* God's child. "…because you [really] are [His] sons, God has sent the [Holy] Spirit of His Son into our hearts, crying, Abba (Father)! Father!" (Galatians 4:6 AMP)

The word "Abba" in this verse is similar to the word "Daddy" in the English language. God is your "Daddy." He speaks to you lovingly just as loving parents on earth speak to their children. He definitely wants you to learn how to hear everything that He is saying to you.

Your Father wants to give you loving guidance each day just as loving parents on earth guide their children and help them. All that your Father asks is that you learn how to hear what He is saying to you. God said, "Oh, that My people would listen to Me, that Israel would walk in My ways!" (Psalm 81:13 AMP)

Just as God wanted the Israelites to listen to Him and to obey His instructions, your Father wants you to listen to Him and to obey His instructions. *Do you* believe that the God of the universe really speaks to *you* every day of your life? If you do believe this great spiritual truth, you should be highly motivated to learn exactly what God instructs you to do to hear what He is saying to you.

Do you have a deep, strong and fervent desire to hear what your Father is saying to you? If you answer this question affirmatively, you will be in a spiritual position where you will be able to learn how to hear what God is saying to you.

There is a definite relationship between the degree of your desire to hear God's voice and how often you will hear what He is saying to you. You should place the same emphasis on hearing what God says as Job did when he said, "I have not gone back from the commandment of His lips; I have esteemed and treasured the words of His mouth more than my necessary food." (Job 23:12 AMP)

You will starve if you go indefinitely without eating food. Hearing God's voice is *more* important to you in the spiritual realm than feeding your body is in the natural realm. Give hearing God's voice the high priority that it deserves.

Learning how to hear God's voice is an absolute necessity. Sometimes just one thing that God will say to you will transform the remainder of your life. We make this statement from personal experience.

Make the quality decision that you *will* pay the price to learn all of the scriptural instructions that will enable you to hear everything that God is saying to you. Assume that God only speaks to you 5 times each day. We can tell you from personal experience that God speaks much more often than 5 times each day. However, if you multiply 5 by 365 days in a year, you will see that God speaks to you *more than 1,800 times each year.*

Using these figures, you can see that God will speak to you almost 200,000 times in a 10-year period. Think of how much longer you have to live based on normal life expectancy for your age. Understand the tens of thousands of times that you will hear God speaking to *you* if you learn how to hear His voice.

Do not make the mistake that many Christians make of putting *anything* ahead of learning how to hear the voice of God. The more that you hear God's voice, the more you will want to hear what your Father is saying to you.

The scriptural principles that we will explain in this book are life-changing. You cannot even begin to comprehend the transformation that will take place in your life *if* you learn how to hear what God is saying to you. There will not be any resemblance between your life before you heard God's voice and your life after you consistently hear God speaking to you.

You will experience meaning and fulfillment in your life that is beyond comprehension when and if you are able to hear God speaking to you several times each day. There are no words in our human vocabulary that can describe the magnificent blessing that you will receive if you consistently hear God speaking to you throughout the remainder of your life.

Chapter 4

God Will Teach You and Encourage You

Your Father has tremendous compassion for you and for all of His other children. "It is because of the Lord's mercy and loving-kindness that we are not consumed, because His [tender] compassions fail not. They are new every morning…" (Lamentations 3:22-23 AMP)

Your Father is kind, loving and merciful. He has continual compassion for you. If you wonder why God desires to speak to you, you must understand that God loves you just as much as He loves His Son. Jesus said, "…You have loved them [even] as You have loved Me." (John 17:23 AMP)

Jesus said these words to His disciples. God loves you just as much as He loved Jesus and just as much as He loved His disciples. Every aspect of your life should be solidly anchored on your deep and constant awareness of God's incredible love for you. "…I pray that you, being rooted and established in love, may have power, together with all the Lord's holy people, to grasp how wide and long and high and deep is the love of Christ, and to know this love that surpasses knowledge – that you may be filled to the measure of all the fullness of God." (Ephesians 3:17-19 NIV)

Please note the words "surpasses knowledge" in this passage of Scripture. The apostle Paul prayed that the Ephesians would grasp the magnitude of the love of Christ. This same love is available to you. Your faith in God should be deeply rooted in your awareness of His love for you. "Though the mountains be shaken and the hills be removed, yet my unfailing love for you will not be shaken nor my covenant of peace be removed," says the Lord, who has compassion on you."(Isaiah 54:10 NIV)

God's love for you is *so* great that nothing can shake His love. Even though you face problems that are so powerful that the magnitude of these problems could shake mountains and remove hills, nothing can cause God's love for you to vary in the slightest. You can have deep, strong and unwavering faith in your Father's love for you.

Your Father's love for you is much greater than the love that any human parent has for his or her children. Do you talk often with the people you love the most? Of course you do. God is no different. He speaks to you often because He loves you.

Your Father will guide you and help you when He talks to you. He loves you so much that He has given you His Book of Instructions, the Bible, to encourage you. "…whatever was thus written in former days was written for our instruction, that by [our steadfast and patient] endurance and the encouragement [drawn] from the Scriptures we might hold fast to and cherish hope." (Romans 15:4 AMP)

Your Father has given you the Bible to help you to be patient and persevering. He has given you the Bible to encourage you. The next verse goes on to refer to your Father as "…God Who gives the power of patient endurance (steadfastness) and Who supplies encouragement…" (Romans 15:5 AMP)

When you face seemingly severe problems, your Father will help you. He will encourage you. The Bible speaks of "…God, Who comforts and encourages and refreshes and cheers the depressed and the sinking…" (II Corinthians 7:6 AMP)

If you are tempted to be discouraged and depressed, God will comfort you and encourage you. You will receive His comfort and encouragement if you learn how to hear His voice.

Jesus Christ is your example in every area. Jesus said, "I am able to do nothing from Myself [independently, of My own accord – but only as I am taught by God and as I get His orders]..." (John 5:30 AMP)

Jesus knew that He could overcome the difficult problems He faced only to the degree that He was taught by God. As Jesus heard His Father's voice, He was able to do what God instructed Him to do. If you are able to hear God's voice, your Father will teach you just as He taught Jesus. Jesus said, "…they shall all be taught of God [have Him in person for their Teacher]…." (John 6:45 AMP)

Please note the word "all" in this verse. This word includes you. God is your Teacher. He speaks to you continually telling you exactly what you should do. God said, "…I am the Lord your God, who teaches you what is best for you, who directs you in the way you should go." (Isaiah 48:17 NIV)

God teaches you by speaking to you. He directs you by the words that He speaks to you. The following prophetic words that Isaiah spoke regarding Jesus Christ apply to your life today if Jesus is your Savior. "…He wakens Me morning by morning, He wakens My ear to hear as a disciple [as one who is taught]." (Isaiah 50:4 AMP)

God taught Jesus throughout His earthly ministry from early in the morning until late at night. Your Father will teach you throughout every day and night of your life. He said, "I [the Lord] will instruct you and teach you in the way you should go; I will counsel you with My eye upon you." (Psalm 32:8 AMP)

If you truly believe that God will teach you, you should praise Him and thank Him continually. You should be like the psalmist who said, "My lips shall pour forth praise [with thanksgiving and renewed trust] when You teach me Your statutes." (Psalm 119:171 AMP)

The Bible is God's Book of Instructions. God is your Teacher. Praise your Father and thank Him for teaching you.

Jesus did not pursue personal desires during His earthly ministry. He based every aspect of His life on what His Father taught Him. Jesus said, "…I do nothing of Myself (of My own accord or on My own authority), but I say [exactly] what My Father has taught Me." (John 8:28 AMP)

Please note that Jesus said and did exactly what God taught Him to say and do. Jesus is your example. You will be blessed abundantly if you hear what God is teaching you and you obey His instructions.

Your Father wants to you to be humble and teachable. He wants you to hear what He is saying to you. Learning to hear God's voice is vitally important to you.

In this chapter we have studied Scripture explaining how much God loves you, that God will encourage you and that God will teach you. In the next chapter we will look into the Word of God for additional information that will show you exactly how your Father will help you if you learn how to hear His voice.

Chapter 5

God Will Guide You Continually

In the following verse of Scripture you will see that God promises to be both your Teacher and your guide. "…your Teacher will not hide Himself any more, but your eyes will constantly behold your Teacher. And your ears will hear a word behind you, saying, This is the way; walk in it, when you turn to the right hand and when you turn to the left." (Isaiah 30:20-21 AMP)

When this verse speaks of your ears hearing a word behind you, the word "behind" refers to the Old Testament primarily emphasizing that God is with you at all times. The New Testament emphasizes that God is *in* you. If Jesus is your Savior, your Teacher lives in your heart. He speaks from within you, not from outside of you.

This verse says that God will tell you when to turn to the right and when to turn to the left. He will speak to you continually to guide you throughout your life on earth. "For this God is our God forever and ever; He will be our guide [even] until death." (Psalm 48:14 AMP)

God promises to guide you throughout your life right up to the day that you die and go to be with Him in heaven. If you learn how to hear God's voice, you will receive constant guidance from Him. "The steps of a [good] man are directed and established by the Lord when He delights in his way [and He busies Himself with his every step]." (Psalm 37:23 AMP)

Once again God promises to direct your steps. Your Father delights in helping you. He "busies Himself" with every step that you take. There is no question that God will guide you and help you. The psalmist understood this great spiritual truth. He said, "…I am continually with You; You do hold my right hand. You will guide me with Your counsel..." (Psalm 73:23-24 AMP)

Little children are secure when one of their loving parents guides them across a busy street by holding their hands. This same principle applies to your life today. Your heavenly Father will hold your hand in the spiritual realm just as He held the hand of the psalmist many years ago.

God promises that He is always with you. You should trust Him to guide you just as little children trust their loving parents. "A man's mind plans his way, but the Lord directs his steps and makes them sure." (Proverbs 16:9 AMP)

Trust God to direct your steps throughout every day of your life. Turn away from selfish desires. Learn to hear what God is saying to you. "…the Lord shall guide you continually..." (Isaiah 58:11 AMP)

Please note the word "continually" in this verse. God guides you by speaking to you. He will speak to you continually, telling you exactly what to do, when to do it and how to do it.

God directed Jesus throughout His earthly ministry by speaking to Him continually. God will direct you the same way. "He delivers the afflicted in their affliction and opens their ears [to His voice] in adversity." (Job 36:15 AMP)

Please note that God promises to open your ears to hear His voice when you face adversity. Are you facing difficult problems? *Expect* God to speak to you. Listen to what He is saying to you. Do what He instructs you to do. God knows exactly what to do when you do not know what to do. He will help you when you face adversity (see Psalm 121:2, Isaiah 41:13 and Hebrews 4:16 and 13:6).

The Bible also teaches that God will give you the right words to say when you need them. When you face adversity and you do not know what to say, God knows exactly what to say. The following words that He spoke to Moses apply to your life today. God said, "Now therefore go, and I will be with your mouth and will teach you what you shall say." (Exodus 4:12 AMP)

When Moses was first appointed as the leader of Israel, he felt incapable of carrying out some of his duties. God assured Moses that He was with him and that He would speak to him and through him. You can trust God completely to give you the words that you need when you need them. "…from the Lord comes the [wise] answer of the tongue." (Proverbs 16:1 AMP)

God will speak to you and through you by giving you the exact words that you need when you do not know what to say. Jesus said, "…do not be anxious about how or what you are to speak; for what you are to say will be given you in that very hour and moment, for it is not you who are speaking, but the Spirit of your Father speaking through you." (Matthew 10:19-20 AMP)

You do not have to worry about what to say when you face a difficult challenge. God will speak through you. Open your mouth. Trust God to speak through you just as He promises.

I have enjoyed this magnificent experience many times in my life. I cannot tell you how many times I have heard myself speaking words that I had no knowledge of beforehand. My human vocabulary is insufficient to explain how excited I have been on numerous occasions when I knew that the God of the universe was speaking through me.

God speaks through you by the Holy Spirit. You *can* trust God to give you the exact words that you need. Open your mouth. Allow the Holy Spirit to speak through you. Trust Him completely to give you the exact words that you need. As this process continues over a period of months and years, you will turn more and more to the Holy Spirit. You will trust Him to speak in you, to you and through you.

God cares about every minute detail in your life. When you do not know what to do, you can go to your loving Father to ask Him for the wisdom that you need. "If any of you is deficient in wisdom, let him ask of the giving God [Who gives] to everyone liberally and ungrudgingly, without reproaching or faultfinding, and it will be given him." (James 1:5 AMP)

Please note that God promises to give wisdom to *everyone*. The word "everyone" includes you. God will not withhold His wisdom from you because of mistakes that you have made. If you have a humble and teachable heart, God will not find fault with you. He will give you wisdom.

We live in uncertain times. We do not know what will happen in the future. However, if Jesus Christ is your Savior, the Holy Spirit Who lives in your heart knows exactly what will happen in the future. Jesus said, "…when He, the Spirit of Truth (the Truth-giving Spirit) comes, He will guide you into all the Truth (the whole, full Truth). For He will not speak His own message [on His own authority]; but He will tell whatever He hears [from the Father; He will give the message that has been given to Him], and He will announce and declare to you the things that are to come [that will happen in the future]." (John 16:13 AMP)

You can be certain that the Holy Spirit Who lives in your heart knows exactly what will happen in the future. He will tell you what to do. Trust Him completely to guide you. Do what He instructs you to do.

In this chapter we have studied several verses of Scripture to assure you that God will guide you. You have seen that God promises to guide you when you face adversity. You have seen that God will give you the answer you need when you do not have the answer. You have seen that God will give you wisdom. You have seen that the Holy Spirit will speak to you and give you important information about what will happen in the future.

Chapter 6

Expect to Hear God Speaking to You

In the first five chapters of this book you have learned that God is omnipresent. He is able to have individual conversations with billions of people all over the world at the same time. If Jesus Christ is your Savior, you can be certain that the same God Who created you and every other person and everything in the universe is talking to *you* throughout every day of your life.

If Jesus is your Savior, God is your Father. You are His beloved child. He loves you unconditionally regardless of any faults or shortcomings that you may have (Please go now to the Appendix at the end of this book if you are not certain that Jesus Christ is your Savior.)

You have learned that God will teach you, guide you, encourage you and help you as He talks with you. Now that you have learned what God will do in regard to speaking to you, we will explain how you can learn to hear God's voice.

God speaks continually to every one of His children. Many of God's children are not listening. *You decide* whether you will hear God speaking to you or not. There is a direct relationship between believing that God really does speak to you and hearing God's voice.

You should *expect* to hear God's voice. You have read many verses of Scripture in this book that assure you that God does speak to you. Do not block yourself from hearing the precious words that God speaks because of doubt and unbelief. "…brethren, take care, lest there be in any one of you a wicked, unbelieving heart [which refuses to cleave to, trust in, and rely on Him], leading you to turn away and desert or stand aloof from the living God." (Hebrews 3:12 AMP)

These words that were spoken to members of the early church apply to your life today. Do not turn away from hearing God because of unbelief. *Know* that God does speak to you continually. Jesus said, "…it shall be done for you as you have believed…." (Matthew 8:13 AMP)

Your faith that God really does speak to you often is the determining factor in hearing God's voice. You should follow the advice of the psalmist David who said, "Wait and hope for and expect the Lord; be brave and of good courage and let your heart be stout and enduring. Yes, wait for and hope for and expect the Lord." (Psalm 27:14 AMP)

This verse begins and ends with the *same* instructions telling you to expect the Lord. You should expect God to do what He promises to do in every area of your life, including speaking to you continually. You should be like the psalmist who said, "I will listen [with expectancy] to what God the Lord will say…" (Psalm 85:8 AMP)

Once again you are instructed to *expect* God to speak to you. Your faith that God is speaking to you is very important. The determining factor in regard to hearing God's voice often is your expectation that God *will* speak to you.

We see an example of this principle in the following story about God speaking to a young boy named Samuel who eventually became a prophet. Samuel had been talking to a man named Eli. After their conversation, Samuel lay down on his bed. "…Samuel was lying down when the Lord called, Samuel! And he answered, Here I am. He ran to Eli and said, Here I am, for you called me. Eli said, I did not call you; lie down again. So he went and lay down." (I Samuel 3:3-5 AMP)

The Lord spoke to Samuel, but Samuel thought that Eli had spoken to him. He went back to bed. "And the Lord called again, Samuel! And Samuel arose and went to Eli and said, Here am I; you did call me. Eli answered, I did not call, my son; lie down again. Now Samuel did not yet know the Lord, and the word of the Lord was not yet revealed to him." (I Samuel 3:6-7 AMP)

God spoke to Samuel a second time. Samuel again thought that Eli was speaking to him. "And the Lord called Samuel the third time. And he went to Eli and said, Here I am, for you did call me. Then Eli perceived that the Lord was calling the boy. So Eli said to Samuel, Go, lie down. And if He calls you, you shall say, Speak, Lord, for Your servant is listening. So Samuel went and lay down in his place." (I Samuel 3:8-9 AMP)

Eli told Samuel that he was hearing the Lord, not him. Finally, Samuel *expected* God to speak to him. "And the Lord came and stood and called as at other times, Samuel! Samuel! Then Samuel answered, Speak, Lord, for Your servant is listening." (I Samuel 3:10 AMP)

You should have this same expectancy. Know that God is speaking to you many times throughout every day of your life. Say to Him, "Speak, Lord, for Your servant is listening."

Your Father will bless you abundantly if you consistently expect Him to speak to you. "Hear instruction and be wise, and do not refuse or neglect it. Blessed (happy, fortunate, to be envied) is the man who listens to me, watching daily at my gates, waiting at the posts of my doors." (Proverbs 8:33-34 AMP)

If you are wise, you *will* listen to what God is telling you. You will not neglect hearing what He is saying. God blesses every one of His children who obey His instructions to listen every day for His voice.

The words that King Solomon spoke to his son in Proverbs 8:33-34 apply to your life today. Please note the use of the word "daily" in this passage of Scripture. Your Father emphasizes the importance of listening for Him to speak to you throughout every day of your life. God said, "Incline your ear [submit and consent to the divine will] and come to Me; hear, and your soul will revive..." (Isaiah 55:3 AMP)

When you incline your ear toward God, you expect to hear Him speaking to you. Your life will be transformed if you consistently hear God's voice. Every aspect of your life should revolve around your absolute certainty that God really does speak to you throughout each day of your life.

God searches the world continually looking for His children who expect to hear His voice. "For the eyes of the Lord run to and fro throughout the whole earth to show Himself strong in behalf of those whose hearts are blameless toward Him..." (II Chronicles 16:9 AMP)

This verse applies to many areas of your life, but it does include hearing what God is saying to you. God is very interested in your learning how to hear what He is saying. He said, "Call to Me and I will answer you and show you great and mighty things, fenced in and hidden, which you do not know (do not distinguish and recognize, have knowledge of and understand)." (Jeremiah 33:3 AMP)

Your Father will show you great and mighty things throughout each day of your life if you expect to hear Him speaking to you. God created you to hear His voice. Your Father does not want you to go through life trying to figure everything out with the limitations of your human understanding. He wants you to learn how to hear what He is saying and then to do what He instructs you to do.

Most human beings are focused on what is taking place in the world. Hearing God's voice does not come naturally to us. This book is filled with numerous scriptural instructions that will enable you to hear what God is saying to you.

God has done His part. He speaks to you continually. He has given you specific instructions telling you how to hear what He is saying. You must do your part. You should be *highly motivated* to learn and obey these instructions that God has given to you.

If you can understand the immensity of the privilege that you have been given to actually hear the Creator of the universe speaking to you, learning how to hear what God is saying will have a very high priority in your life. You should be willing to pay a significant price to study and meditate on God's specific instructions about hearing His voice.

Hearing God's voice is somewhat analogous to the ability to tune in to a radio or television program. At this very moment many radio stations and television channels are broadcasting in the atmosphere around you. You can only hear these voices if you know how to tune in to a designated frequency on a radio station or a specific television channel.

You probably have experienced trying to tune in to a radio station and hearing a lot of static. The static in the spiritual realm comes from the things of the world that draw your attention away from being able to tune into and hear God's voice. The static in the spiritual realm often comes from Satan's demons doing everything that they can to influence you to pursue other goals so that you will not pay the price of learning how to tune in to the voice of God. "Take firm hold of instruction, do not let go; guard her, for she is your life." (Proverbs 4:13 AMP)

This verse applies to instructions in the Bible. These instructions also include learning how to hear God's voice. Hold tightly onto the scriptural instructions that we are giving you in this book. Make a firm commitment to learn and to obey God's specific instructions in regard to hearing His voice. Your life will be *transformed* if you do.

You learn how to hear God's voice progressively. The more you hear God's voice, the more you will desire to hear God's voice. As the days turn into weeks, the weeks turn into months and the months turn into years and you learn and obey the specific instructions that God has given to you, you will find yourself hearing His voice more clearly throughout every day of your life.

Chapter 7

Intimacy with God and Hearing God's Voice

In this chapter we will look into God's Word for additional information that will help you to hear God speaking to you. The one question that Christians ask above every other question in this area is how they can be certain that the voice they hear is the voice of God.

Jesus Christ gave us the answer to this question when He said, "…he who enters by the door is the shepherd of the sheep. The watchman opens the door for this man, and the sheep listen to his voice and heed it; and he calls his own sheep by name and brings (leads) them out. When he has brought his own sheep outside, he walks on before them, and the sheep follow him because they know his voice. They will never [on any account] follow a stranger, but will run away from him because they do not know the voice of strangers or recognize their call." (John 10:2-5 AMP)

You can clearly identify the voice of God just as sheep know the voice of their shepherd. Sheep are inadequate in many areas. They live by instinct. They trust their shepherd completely. They know his voice based on a long and close relationship with him. They do what their shepherd tells them to do.

If you truly have an intimate relationship with God, you will know His voice. Jesus explained this principle when He said, "The sheep that are My own hear and are listening to My voice; and I know them, and they follow Me." (John 10:27 AMP)

If Jesus is your Savior, He is your Shepherd. Because Jesus is your Shepherd, you can be certain that you *can* hear Him speaking to you just as sheep know the voice of their shepherd.

A sheep that has been part of a flock for many years can hear the voice of its shepherd much more clearly than a newborn lamb. This same principle applies to hearing God's voice. If you have spent many years drawing closer to God, you will hear His voice more clearly than a Christian who has spent little or no time drawing close to God.

There is a direct relationship between how well you know another person in the world and your ability to identify this person's voice. Please stop and think of the members of your immediate family and other people who are close to you. If you receive a telephone call from any of these people, they do not have to identify themselves. You do not need caller ID. You will instantly know the voice of each of these people because of your intimate long-term relationship with them.

This same principle applies to hearing God's voice. You should become more familiar with God's voice than you are with the voice of any person in the world. If you consistently draw closer to God, you will have no doubt that the voice you are hearing is the voice of God.

Some Christians are similar to Pharisees. They are religious people who go to church once or twice each week out of a sense of duty. These Christians pray briefly each day. They do their best to live a moral lifestyle.

If Jesus Christ is the Savior of people who live this way, they will live throughout eternity in heaven. However, many casual Christians are very preoccupied with things in the world that block them from hearing God's voice. Casual Christians do not hear the voice of God. Only committed believers hear the voice of God.

If you have a distant relationship with God or no relationship at all, He will speak to you each day but you will not hear Him. God does not want a long-distance relationship with you. He wants to have a close and intimate relationship with each of His beloved children.

We will not attempt to give you a formula that will enable you to hear God's voice. You will not hear God's voice if you try an intellectual approach to hearing Him. You only will be able to hear God's voice to the degree of the intimacy of your relationship with Him.

You do not hear the voice of God each day with your physical ears. You hear God in your heart with the spiritual ears of the hidden person who lives in your heart – the real you (see I Peter 3:4).

You develop an intimate relationship with a person on earth by spending a significant amount of time with this person. This same principle applies to God. You develop an intimate relationship with God by spending a significant amount of time with Him each and every day.

Many Christians who will live eternally in heaven do not enjoy a close and intimate relationship with God on earth. They do not learn and obey the instructions that God has given to us that enable us to draw closer to Him. "Behold, God is great, and we know Him not!..." (Job 36:26 AMP)

In the first two chapters we explained that the Creator of the universe wants you to hear Him talking with *you* throughout every day of your life. We explained that God is omnipresent. He is fully able to have billions of simultaneous conversations with people all over the world.

God *is* great. Learn and obey God's instructions to draw closer to Him. Do not be like the Pharisees that Jesus spoke of when He said, "...These people [constantly] honor Me with their lips, but their hearts hold off and are far distant from Me." (Mark 7:6 AMP)

The Pharisees were religious people. They attempted to make a good impression on other people because of their religious lifestyle. However, as Jesus said, the hearts of the Pharisees were far away from Him. Your heart is the key to an intimate relationship with God (see Proverbs 23:7).

You should take full advantage of the precious privilege that Jesus Christ has given to every person who has received Him as his or her Savior. "…the Son of God has [actually] come to this world and has given us understanding and insight [progressively] to perceive (recognize) and come to know better and more clearly Him Who is true…" (I John 5:20 AMP)

Jesus left the glory of heaven and came to earth to give *you* the opportunity to progressively know God more intimately. God has told you exactly what to do to develop a close relationship with Him. "Come close to God and He will come close to you.…" (James 4:8 AMP)

God does not initiate the contact with you. *You* initiate the contact with God. If you learn and consistently obey God's instructions to come close to Him, you can be certain that your loving Father *will* come close to you.

Many of the promises in the Bible are conditional. God will do what He promises to do if you do what He instructs you to do. You should do your very best to come close to God on a regular and consistent basis. If you do, there is no question that God *will* come closer to you.

You decide how close you will be to God. *You decide* how clearly and how often you will hear His voice. God's decision already has been made. God talks to every one of His children continually. The question is not whether God is talking to you, but whether you will learn how to hear what He is saying.

You can only hear what God is saying to you to the degree that you consistently turn away from all of the distractions in the world to draw closer to Him. As you consistently turn away from the world and draw closer to God, you will become one with

Him. "...the person who is united to the Lord becomes one spirit with Him." (I Corinthians 6:17 AMP)

Are you united to God? Are you one with God? Does the following verse of Scripture describe your personal relationship with God? "You shall walk after the Lord your God and [reverently] fear Him, and keep His commandments and obey His voice, and you shall serve Him and cling to Him." (Deuteronomy 13:4 AMP)

This verse instructs you to fear God. When you fear God, you hold Him in constant reverence and awe. Every aspect of your life revolves around Him. You consistently study His Word and obey the instructions that He has given to you. As you do these things over a period of time, you will learn to hear His voice. "...let us be zealous to know the Lord [to appreciate, give heed to, and cherish Him]...." (Hosea 6:3 AMP)

This verse of Scripture instructs you to be *zealous* to know God. When people are zealous, they are totally committed to whatever they are doing. You should be completely devoted to developing a more intimate relationship with God. The amplification of this verse says that you should "appreciate the Lord, give heed to Him and cherish Him." "...whoever would come near to God must [necessarily] believe that God exists and that He is the rewarder of those who earnestly and diligently seek Him [out]." (Hebrews 11:6 AMP)

All Christians believe that God exists. You must do more than just acknowledge the existence of God. You must understand that God *will* reward you *if* you seek Him "earnestly and diligently."

Your Father does not want you to have a casual attitude toward Him. He wants you to have a deep and sincere desire to know Him intimately and to hear His voice continually. Your Father wants you to be totally committed to drawing closer to Him. "...you must abide in (live in, never depart from) Him [being rooted in Him, knit to Him]..." (I John 2:27 AMP)

This verse instructs you to abide in God. When you abide in God, you keep Him in first place in your life at all times. The amplification says that you should "live in and never depart from" God. Your relationship with God should be deeply rooted. You should have a closely knit and intimate relationship with God.

Do these words describe your relationship with God? Is He at the center of your life? Does every aspect of your life revolve around Him? If you truly desire to hear God speaking to you, these words should describe your relationship with God.

Chapter 8

Program Yourself to Hear God's Voice

God speaks to all of His children through His written Word. The Bible contains general instructions for every child of God. If you consistently study and obey these general instructions, you will be much more likely to hear God's voice with the specific instructions that He has for you.

If you study and meditate on the Word of God each day, you will turn more and more away from the world and turn toward God. "…He has bestowed on us His precious and exceedingly great promises, so that through them you may escape [by flight] from the moral decay (rottenness and corruption) that is in the world because of covetousness (lust and greed), and become sharers (partakers) of the divine nature." (II Peter 1:4 AMP)

You cannot hear God's voice if you are primarily tuned in to the world. Please note that this verse and the amplification speak of the "moral decay, rottenness and corruption" that pervades the world as a result of greed and selfishness. If you consistently fill your mind and your heart with the Word of God, you actually will partake of the nature of God. You will become more and more like God.

Christians cannot consistently hear God's voice without faithfully obeying His instructions to renew their minds by studying His Word every day (see II Corinthians 4:16 and Ephesians 4:23) and meditating day and night on the holy Scriptures (see Joshua 1:8 and Psalm 1:2-3). Christians who either do not know or disobey these specific instructions from God will block themselves from hearing the voice of God.

Every word in the Bible is inspired by God. The divine origin of God's Book of Instructions enables you to tune in to His voice. "All scripture is given by inspiration of God, and is profitable for doctrine, for reproof, for correction, for instruction in righteousness: That the man of God may be perfect, thoroughly furnished unto all good works." (II Timothy 3:16-17 KJV)

The Bible is completely different from any other book. All other books are written by human authors. God is the Author of the Bible. The Bible is filled with the supernatural power of God. "…the Word that God speaks is alive and full of power [making it active, operative, energizing, and effective]; it is sharper than any two-edged sword, penetrating to the dividing line of the breath of life (soul) and [the immortal] spirit, and of joints and marrow [of the deepest parts of our nature], exposing and sifting and analyzing and judging the very thoughts and purposes of the heart." (Hebrews 4:12 AMP)

The Word of God has a spiritual life of its own. It is filled to overflowing with God's supernatural power. The Word of God will energize you. It will penetrate deep down inside of you, helping you to understand yourself better.

You will program yourself with instructions from God that fill your mind and your heart with the power of God if you consistently study and meditate on His Word. "…you received the message of God [which you heard] from us, you welcomed it not as the word of [mere] men, but as it truly is, the Word of God, which is effectually at work in you who believe [exercising its superhuman power in those who adhere to and trust in and rely on it]." (I Thessalonians 2:13 AMP)

Once again you are told that the Bible is "*not* the voice of mere men." God supernaturally anointed each of the human authors of the Bible. He gave them divinely inspired promises and instructions that will release His supernatural power in your life to the degree that you obey His instructions and have absolute faith that He will fulfill His promises.

Jesus Christ explained the relationship between knowing the Word of God and hearing God's voice. The following words that Jesus spoke to Pontius Pilate many years ago apply to you today. Jesus said, "…Everyone who is of the Truth [who is a friend of the Truth, who belongs to the Truth] hears and listens to My voice." (John 18:37 AMP)

When Jesus speaks of the Truth, He refers to the Word of God (see John 17:17). You will hear Jesus speaking to you in direct proportion to the degree that you consistently study and meditate on the Word of God.

If you are a friend of the Truth and you belong to the Truth, you will hunger and thirst for the Word of God. You will not be able to get enough of it. The more of God's Word that you get, the more you will want. Jesus said, "Sky and earth will pass away, but My words will not pass away." (Matthew 24:35 AMP)

Jesus says here that the Word of God will outlive the world that you live in and the sky that is above you. Everything in the world is temporary. The Word of God is *eternal*. The Bible refers to itself as "…the ever living and lasting Word of God." (I Peter 1:23 AMP)

Books that are written by human beings are temporary because of their human origin. The Word of God is eternal because of its divine origin. Jesus said, "Sanctify them [purify, consecrate, separate them for Yourself, make them holy] by the Truth; Your Word is Truth." (John 17:17 AMP)

The amplification of this verse explains that sanctification is purifying yourself and separating yourself from the world. You will become more like God if you consistently fill your mind and your heart with the Truth of His Word. Jesus said, "…you will know the Truth, and the Truth will set you free." (John 8:32 AMP)

The Truth of the Word of God can set you free from anything that is blocking you from hearing what God is saying to you. "…the mind of the flesh [with its carnal thoughts and purposes] is hostile to God, for it does not submit itself to God's Law; indeed it cannot. So then those who are living the life of the flesh [catering to the appetites and impulses of their carnal nature] cannot please or satisfy God, or be acceptable to Him." (Romans 8:7-8 AMP)

Worldly thinking is hostile to God. People who are worldly-oriented do not obey God's instructions. Worldly thinking blocks you from hearing God's voice because worldly thinking revolves around self-centeredness and the ways of the world.

Jesus told the Pharisees why they did not hear God's voice. He said, "…the Father Who sent Me has Himself testified concerning Me. Not one of you has ever given ear to His voice or seen His form (His face – what He is like). [You have always been deaf to His voice and blind to the vision of Him.] And you have not His word (His thought) living in your hearts, because you do not believe and adhere to and trust in and rely on Him Whom He has sent. [That is why you do not keep His message living in you, because you do not believe in the Messenger Whom He has sent.]" (John 5:37-38 AMP)

Jesus explained that the Pharisees were unable to hear the voice of God because they did not believe in Him. God sent Jesus to earth. Keep Jesus Christ as the focus of your life. Without Him, the Word of God will not be powerful to you.

If you study and meditate each day on the Word of God as your Father has instructed you to do, you will program yourself to hear God's voice. You will program yourself in a way that is similar to programming a computer. You are able to hear God speaking to you to the degree that you have programmed yourself with specific instructions and promises that come directly from God. You are charging yourself with the supernatural power of God.

You cannot be certain that God is talking to you and that you are not just making up words if you have not spent a considerable amount of time in God's Word. If your mind and your heart are filled with God's Word, the words that you hear always will line up with the Word of God.

The amount of God's Word that lives in your mind and your heart is cumulative. If you have spent many months and years studying and meditating on the Word of God, you have a substantial reservoir of God's Word in your mind and your heart. You have programmed yourself over a long period of time to enable yourself to hear God speaking to you.

In this chapter we have established a scriptural foundation to explain the relationship that exists between consistently studying and meditating on the Word of God and hearing the voice of God. In the next two chapters we will look into the holy Scriptures for more instruction about the absolute necessity of consistently studying and meditating on God's Word and hearing the voice of God.

Chapter 9

Are You in Awe of the Word of God?

If you are absolutely certain that every word in the Bible is inspired by God, you will be in absolute awe of the Word of God. If you know that the Word of God is eternal, you should revere God's Word just as you revere God Himself. You should be like the psalmist who said, "…my heart stands in awe of Your words…" (Psalm 119:161 AMP)

Your awe of God and His Word will increase in direct proportion to the amount of God's Word that abides in your mind and your heart. If you faithfully study and meditate on the holy Scriptures, you will revere the Word of God. "…he who [reverently] fears and respects the commandment [of God] is rewarded." (Proverbs 13:13 AMP)

Your Father promises to reward you if you revere His Word because you have so much awe and respect for His Word. One way that God will reward you is by enabling you to hear His voice because you have faithfully obeyed His instructions to consistently study and meditate on His Word. God said, "…this is the man to whom I will look and have regard: he who is humble and of a broken or wounded spirit, and who trembles at My word and reveres My commands." (Isaiah 66:2 AMP)

God explains exactly what type of person He seeks. He is looking for His children who are humble and teachable. Do you *tremble* at the Word of God? Do you *revere* the Word of God? If these words describe your attitude toward the holy Scriptures, you will constantly be programming yourself to hear the voice of God. Shortly after what God said in Isaiah 66:2, He repeated this instruction when He said, "Hear the word of the Lord, you who tremble at His word…" (Isaiah 66:5 AMP)

This short verse explains the relationship between *hearing* God's Word and being in awe of the holy Scriptures. If you revere God's Word, you actually will tremble in the spiritual realm before God's Word just as you would tremble if God Himself suddenly appeared before you.

You cannot understand God's ways through the limitations of human logic, reasoning and understanding. God's ways are very different from the ways of the world. "…My thoughts are not your thoughts, neither are your ways My ways, says the Lord. For as the heavens are higher than the earth, so are My ways higher than your ways and My thoughts than your thoughts." (Isaiah 55:8-9 AMP)

God does not think the way that worldly people think. God's ways are much higher than the ways of the world. God's thoughts are much higher than the thoughts of the world.

Sometimes God will instruct you to do something that makes no sense from the perspective of worldly logic and reasoning. However, if you have consistently programmed yourself with God's Word, you will find that what God is telling you makes perfect sense.

You must be completely open to God speaking to you in ways that are very different from the ways of the world. You must be willing to obey God's instructions if His instructions do not make sense to the limitations of your human logic, understanding and reasoning. "Study and be eager and do your utmost to present yourself to God approved (tested by trial), a workman who has no cause to be ashamed, correctly analyzing and accurately dividing [rightly handling and skillfully teaching] the Word of Truth." (II Timothy 2:15 AMP)

This verse explains that, if you sincerely desire to win God's approval, you will be eager to study His Word. You will work hard each day on your Bible study and Scripture meditation.

We have done a lot of the work for you in this book. We have divided the Word of God into 20 chapters that will give you a thorough scriptural explanation of how to hear the voice of God. Your daily Bible study should be much more effective because you will not have to dig out all of these verses of Scripture yourself.

You will consistently turn away from the ways of the world and program yourself to hear God's voice if you renew your mind each day in the Word of God. "Do not be conformed to this world (this age), [fashioned after and adapted to its external, superficial customs], but be transformed (changed) by the [entire] renewal of your mind [by its new ideals and its new attitude]…" (Romans 12:2 AMP)

The amplification of this verse speaks of the external and superficial ways of the world. You cannot hear God's voice if you consistently put people, places, things and events in the world ahead of God. Your life will be *transformed* if you renew your mind by studying God's Word each day. "Strip yourselves of your former nature [put off and discard your old unrenewed self] which characterized your previous manner of life and becomes corrupt through lusts and desires that spring from delusion; and be constantly renewed in the spirit of your mind [having a fresh mental and spiritual attitude], and put on the new nature (the regenerate self) created in God's image, [Godlike] in true righteousness and holiness." (Ephesians 4:22-24 AMP)

This passage of Scripture instructs you to *strip yourself* of the way that you used to think. You are instructed to *constantly* renew your mind by studying the Word of God. The amplification of this verse says that you will have "a fresh mental and spiritual attitude" if you consistently renew your mind in God's Word. "…Though our outer man is [progressively] decaying and wasting away, yet our inner self is being [progressively] renewed day after day." (II Corinthians 4:16 AMP)

Many people find that their bodies decay and waste away as they grow older because of choices they have made over the years. Older people who are experiencing health challenges must offset the deterioration in their bodies by renewing their minds in God's Word *day after day*.

Please note the word "constantly" in Ephesians 4:23 and "day after day" in II Corinthians 4:16. There is *no* question that your Father wants you to renew your mind by studying His Word each and every day of your life. You will not hear God's voice if you do not consistently renew your mind in His Word.

When you study the Word of God, you fill your mind with God's Word. In the remainder of this chapter we will study instructions that we have shared in almost every book we have ever written. We know from many years of experience that you must *meditate* on the Word of God in addition to your daily Bible study if you truly desire to hear God speaking to you.

If you faithfully obey your Father's instructions to study and meditate daily on His Word, you will be tuned in to hear God's voice. You will be tuned in to God's spiritual wavelength because you have constantly studied and meditated on His Book of Instructions, the Bible. "The entrance and unfolding of Your words give light; their unfolding gives understanding (discernment and comprehension) to the simple." (Psalm 119:130 AMP)

When God's Word consistently enters into your mind and your heart, you will receive supernatural understanding and discernment that you cannot obtain in any other way. "…you shall lay up these My words in your [minds and] hearts and in your [entire] being…" (Deuteronomy 11:18 AMP)

You will store up more and more of God's Word within yourself if you study and meditate daily on the holy Scriptures. "Let the word [spoken by] Christ (the Messiah) have its home [in your hearts and minds] and dwell in you in [all its] richness…" (Colossians 3:16 AMP)

When you fill your mind and your heart with the supernatural living Word of God, you program yourself to obey your Father's instructions. "…the word is very near you, in your mouth and in your mind and in your heart, so that you can do it." (Deuteronomy 30:14 AMP)

We have talked primarily in this chapter about renewing your *mind* by studying God's Word. When you consistently meditate on God's Word, the Scripture that you are meditating on drops from your mind down into your *heart*. The more that you meditate on the Word of God, the more you will desire to meditate on it. You will be like the psalmist who said, "Oh, how love I Your law! It is my meditation all the day." (Psalm 119:97 AMP)

We now are ready to study two very important verses of Scripture pertaining to Scripture meditation that are included in almost every one of our books. We will begin with the instructions that God gave to Joshua when he succeeded Moses as the leader of Israel. God said, "This Book of the Law shall not depart out of your mouth, but you shall meditate on it day and night, that you may observe and do according to all that is written in it. For then you shall make your way prosperous, and then you shall deal wisely and have good success." (Joshua 1:8 AMP)

The instructions that God spoke directly to Joshua many years ago also are His instructions to you. The first part of this verse consists of specific instructions from God to you. The last part explains what God will do in your life *if* you obey the instructions that He has given to you in the first part of the verse.

You are told that the Word of God should not depart out of your mouth. Your ears will hear your voice consistently speaking the Word of God if you faithfully obey God's instructions to *meditate day and night* on His Word. Consistent Scripture meditation programs you to *do* what God instructs you to do.

If you obey these instructions from God, you are told that you will make your way prosperous. The Hebrew word "tsalach" that is translated as "prosperous" in this verse includes much more than financial prosperity. This word means "to push forward, break out and go over."

If you meditate day and night on God's Word, you will break through. You will be able to hear God's voice. You will be able to overcome the problems you face. You will prosper financially.

You will receive wisdom from God as you hear what God is saying to you as a result of meditating day and night on His Word. You will be successful in hearing God's voice and in doing whatever your Father instructs you to do if you obey these specific instructions.

Next we will study the other passage of Scripture pertaining to Scripture meditation that is included in most of our books. "…his delight and desire are in the law of the Lord, and on His law (the precepts, the instructions, the teachings of God) he habitually meditates (ponders and studies) by day and by night. And he shall be like a tree firmly planted [and tended] by the streams of water, ready to bring forth its fruit in its season; its leaf also shall not fade or wither; and everything he does shall prosper [and come to maturity]." (Psalm 1:2-3 AMP)

You should be *delighted* with the Word of God. If you understand the divine origin of the Bible and the eternal existence of the Bible, you will be highly motivated to meditate day and night on God's Word. If you obey these instructions, you will be like a tree that is planted next to a stream of water.

Trees that are planted next to a stream are able to continue to bring forth fruit even though no rain comes down from the sky. These trees continue to produce fruit because their roots are able to bring up water from the stream when there is no rain.

Once again you are told that you will prosper if you meditate day and night on God's Word. The same Hebrew word "tsalach" that we explained in Joshua 1:8 is used here. If you meditate day and night on God's Word, you will produce supernatural spiritual fruit in your life. Hearing God speaking to you continually is one example of the fruit that will be produced in your life if you meditate day and night on the Word of God.

In the last two chapters you have seen that God instructs you to renew your mind daily in His Word and to meditate day and night on His Word. Unfortunately, only a small percentage of Christians renew their minds in God's Word by studying the Word of God daily. Very few Christians meditate day and night on the Word of God even though this is what God has specifically instructed His children to do.

Many Christians attempt to learn the Bible secondhand from preachers and teachers in their churches. You *should* learn from your pastor and teachers in your church, but there is no way that their preaching and teaching should be a substitute for the consistent Bible study and Scripture meditation that God has instructed you to do.

As you meditate day and night on the Word of God, your ears will hear your voice consistently speaking God's Word. There is a direct relationship between your ears hearing your voice speaking the Word of God and hearing God speaking to you.

Chapter 10

Obey God's Instructions

In the last two chapters we have studied the relationship between obeying God's instructions in the Bible and hearing God's voice. In Chapter 4 you learned that God is your Teacher. God teaches you and guides you continually. Are you learning how to hear His teaching and His guidance throughout every day of your life?

In this chapter we will study Scripture that will show you the relationship between obeying God's written instructions, His spoken instructions and consistently hearing His voice. The Bible often does not differentiate between God's written instructions and His spoken instructions. Your Father wants you to do everything that He has told you to do in the Bible and to faithfully obey what He tells you to do when He speaks to you. "Blessed (happy, fortunate, to be envied) are they who keep His testimonies, and who seek, inquire for and of Him and crave Him with the whole heart." (Psalm 119:2 AMP)

God promises to bless His children who obey the instructions He gives in the Bible. Your Father wants you to have a deep yearning to consistently draw closer to Him. If you truly have an intimate relationship with God, you will obey His instructions. "…this is how we may discern [daily, by experience] that we are coming to know Him [to perceive, recognize, understand, and become better acquainted with Him]: if we keep (bear in mind, observe, practice) His teachings (precepts, commandments)." (I John 2:3 AMP)

How can you tell if you are drawing closer to God? This verse explains that you will know God more intimately if you obey His instructions. "Whoever says, I know Him [I perceive, recognize, understand, and am acquainted with Him] but fails to keep and obey His commandments (teachings) is a liar, and the Truth [of the Gospel] is not in him." (I John 2:4 AMP)

You have seen that God's Word is the Truth (see John 17:17). You have learned that your Father instructs you to consistently fill your mind and your heart with His Word. You cannot know God intimately if you do not learn and obey His instructions. God promises to bless you abundantly if you consistently live your life in obedience to His instructions. "…No good thing will He withhold from those who walk uprightly." (Psalm 84:11 AMP)

When this verse instructs you to walk uprightly, this means to live your life in obedience to God's instructions. The words "*no good thing*" in this verse include hearing the voice of God. If you consistently do your best to learn and obey God's instructions, you will place yourself in a spiritual position where you will consistently hear God's voice. "…we receive from Him whatever we ask, because we [watchfully] obey His orders [observe His suggestions and injunctions, follow His plan for us] and [habitually] practice what is pleasing to Him." (I John 3:22 AMP)

The words "whatever we ask" in this verse include hearing God's voice. If you ask God to be able to clearly hear Him speaking to you, He will respond to the degree that you consistently obey His instructions and seek His will for your life. "…be doers of the Word [obey the message], and not merely listeners to it, betraying yourselves [into deception by reasoning contrary to the Truth]." (James 1:22 AMP)

God wants you to do more than just listen to His Word being preached and taught in your church. This verse explains that you will put yourself into a spiritual position where Satan's demons are able to deceive you if your thinking is based on the limitations of human logic and understanding instead of being based on learning and obeying God's instructions.

The following words that God spoke to Moses will apply to your life today if you hear what God is telling you to do and obey His instructions. God said, "…if you will obey My voice in truth and keep My covenant, then you shall be My own peculiar possession and treasure from among and above all peoples…" (Exodus 19:5 AMP)

If you know what God is telling you to do and if you consistently do what He instructs you to do, you will be a *treasure* to God. "If you will listen diligently to the voice of the Lord your God, being watchful to do all His commandments which I command you this day, the Lord your God will set you high above all the nations of the earth. And all these blessings shall come upon you and overtake you if you heed the voice of the Lord your God." (Deuteronomy 28:1-2 AMP)

When this verse instructs you to listen diligently to God's voice, this means that you should place a high priority on hearing God's voice. You should be determined to hear what God is saying and to do what He instructs you to do. "…man does not live by bread only, but man lives by every word that proceeds out of the mouth of the Lord." (Deuteronomy 8:3 AMP)

This verse compares the importance of eating good natural food with doing everything that you hear God instructing you to do. "…the Lord will surely bless you in the land which the Lord your God gives you for an inheritance to possess, if only you carefully listen to the voice of the Lord your God, to do watchfully all these commandments which I command you this day." (Deuteronomy 15:4-5 AMP)

God uses the word "surely" in this passage of Scripture to emphasize that He *definitely* will bless you if you will listen carefully to what He says to you and if you will consistently do what He instructs you to do. You clearly identify yourself as a child of God to the degree that you listen to His voice and then do what He instructs you to do. God said, "…Listen to and obey My voice, and I will be your God and you will be My people; and walk in the whole way that I command you, that it may be well with you." (Jeremiah 7:23 AMP)

This verse consists of instructions that God gave to the Israelites. The Israelites often disobeyed God's instructions. Many of the problems that the Israelites faced came on them because they heard what God was saying to them and they did not do what God instructed them to do. This same principle applies to your life today. "…if you would hear His voice and when you hear it, do not harden your hearts ..." (Hebrews 3:15 AMP)

A humble and teachable heart is essential to hearing God's voice. Do not be hard-hearted. Humble yourself before God by your sincere desire to learn and to do everything that He instructs you to do.

There is a direct relationship between hearing God's instructions, obeying these instructions and hearing more instructions from God. Every time that you act on the instructions that God gives to you, you are much more likely to hear Him giving you additional instructions in the future.

We now are ready to look into God's Word to learn exactly what you should do to show God that you love Him. Before we study these verses of Scripture, ask yourself now how do you believe that you show your love for God? "… the [true] love of God is this: that we do His commands [keep His ordinances and are mindful of His precepts and teaching]. And these orders of His are not irksome (burdensome, oppressive, or grievous)." (I John 5:3 AMP)

If you truly love God, you will *do* what He instructs you to do. God's instructions are not a burden – they are a blessing. Little children show their love for their parents by doing what their parents tell them to do. This same principle applies to your heavenly Father. "…love the Lord your God, obey His voice, and cling to Him. For He is your life and the length of your days…" (Deuteronomy 30:20 AMP)

Your Father repeatedly promises to bless you abundantly if you consistently draw closer to Him and obey the instructions He has given to you. There is a definite relationship between the length and quality of your life and obeying God's instructions. Jesus said, "…there is nothing hidden except to be revealed, nor is anything [temporarily] kept secret except in order that it may be made known. If any man has ears to hear, let him be listening and let him perceive and comprehend." (Mark 4:22-23 AMP)

God wants to reveal great hidden truths to you. Listen to what God tells you. Learn from Him. Do what He tells you to do. Jesus said, "Be careful therefore how you listen. For to him who has [spiritual knowledge] will more be given; and from him who does not have [spiritual knowledge], even what he thinks and guesses and supposes that he has will be taken away." (Luke 8:18 AMP)

Listen carefully to what God tells you to do. If you consistently hear and obey God's instructions, you will grow and mature spiritually. If you do not obey these instructions, you will regress in your spiritual maturity. "…you have become dull in your [spiritual] hearing and sluggish [even slothful in achieving spiritual insight]. For even though by this time you ought to be teaching others, you actually need someone to teach you over again the very first principles of God's Word. You have come to need milk, not solid food." (Hebrews 5:11-12 AMP)

You should be alert to God's voice. You should have a deep desire to hear what God is saying to you and to obey His instructions. Many Christians do not hear God's voice consistently. They should be teaching others, but they still require someone to teach them basic principles pertaining to Christianity.

You have seen that God is able to speak to billions of His children all over the world throughout every day of their lives. God gives specific instructions each day to every one of His children. *Are you* hearing the specific instructions that God is giving to you? *Are you* doing what God instructs you to do?

This chapter is filled with Scripture that tells you to *obey* both God's written and verbal instructions. In the next chapter we will look into God's Word to see the relationship that exists between turning away from the world, drawing closer to God and consistently hearing and obeying God's instructions.

Chapter 11

Turn Away from the Ways of the World

If you faithfully obey the scriptural instructions that we have explained in the first ten chapters of this book, you *will* turn more and more away from the ways of the world. You then will be able to hear the voice of God much more clearly.

This world is not your home. You may be listed as a citizen of a particular country but, if Jesus Christ is your Savior, you actually are a citizen of heaven. "…we are citizens of the state (commonwealth, homeland) which is in heaven…" (Philippians 3:20 AMP)

Heaven is your home. Turn away from the world by consistently immersing yourself in the Word of God. You should be like the psalmist who said, "Open my eyes, that I may behold wondrous things out of Your law. I am a stranger and a temporary resident on the earth; hide not Your commandments from me." (Psalm 119:18-19 AMP)

This passage of Scripture explains that you are only a temporary resident of this world. Pray and ask God to show you supernatural truths as you faithfully obey His instructions to study and meditate on His Word each day. Turn away from the natural realm to consistently learn more and more about the spiritual realm. Jesus explained this principle when He said, "If you belonged to the world, the world would treat you with affection and would love you as its own. But because you are not of the world [no longer one with it], but I have chosen (selected) you out of the world, the world hates (detests) you." (John 15:19 AMP)

Some people in the world look at Christians as being strange because we live by God's standards that are completely different from the ways of the world (see Isaiah 55:8-9). God's Word says that all Christians are "…aliens and strangers and exiles [in this world]…" (I Peter 2:11 AMP)

If Jesus Christ is your Savior, you are an *alien* in this world. You should focus continually on instructions from God instead of living your life based on the ways of the world. "Look carefully then how you walk! Live purposefully and worthily and accurately, not as the unwise and witless, but as wise (sensible, intelligent people), making the very most of the time [buying up each opportunity], because the days are evil." (Ephesians 5:15-16 AMP)

If you pay the price of studying God's Word each day and meditating day and night on the holy Scriptures, your life will line up with God's instructions. You will not live the way that people who know little or nothing of God's Word live. This verse instructs you to look carefully at how you live. Every aspect of your life should line up with the Word of God. Make the most of your time on earth.

This verse says that the days we live in are evil. If you want to hear the voice of God, you must turn away from the world that is so greatly influenced by Satan and his demons. "…the whole world is under the control of the evil one." (I John 5:19 NIV)

Satan has a tremendous influence on the world today. Think about the headlines in the newspaper today compared to the headlines when you were a child. Evil is openly seen and often accepted as good. You will only hear the voice of God to the degree that you consistently turn *away* from the evil that is so dominant in the world. "…consider and look not to the things that are seen but to the things that are unseen; for the things that are visible are temporal (brief and fleeting), but the things that are invisible are deathless and everlasting." (II Corinthians 4:18 AMP)

Turn away from the things of the world that you can see with your eyes and hear with your ears. Learn and obey the great scriptural truths that pertain to the unseen spiritual realm. Everything in the world is temporary. Everything that you learn from the Word of God is eternal (see Psalm 119:96, Isaiah 40:6-8 and Matthew 24:35).

In Chapter 9 we studied Romans 12:2. We studied this verse at that time primarily in regard to renewing your mind in the Word of God. We now would like to look again at a portion of this verse that refers to what we are studying in this chapter. "Do not be conformed to this world (this age), [fashioned after and adapted to its external, superficial customs]…" (Romans 12:2 AMP)

Some Christians are influenced by the superficial ways of the world. They do their best to live a good moral life. They attend church regularly. They pray for a few minutes each day. However, their lives are focused primarily on people and events in the world instead of focusing on God. "…turn not aside from following the Lord, but serve Him with all your heart. And turn not aside after vain and worthless things which cannot profit or deliver you, for they are empty and futile." (I Samuel 12:20-21 AMP)

Turn away from the world to serve God with all your heart. Refuse to live your life based on the "vain, worthless, empty and futile" ways of the world.

Most knowledgeable Christians believe that our generation lives in the last days before the return of Jesus Christ. When the Bible speaks of what people will be like during the last days, it says that they will be "…inflated with self-conceit. [They will be] lovers of sensual pleasures and vain amusements more than and rather than lovers of God." (II Timothy 3:4 AMP)

These words accurately describe many people in our generation. Many people are self-centered, not God-centered. Their primary goal is the pursuit of pleasure. These people place the pursuit of worldly goals ahead of learning and obeying instructions from God. Do not make this mistake. "…Turn away from the irreverent babble and godless chatter, with the vain and empty and worldly phrases, and the subtleties and the contradictions in what is falsely called knowledge and spiritual illumination." (I Timothy 6:20 AMP)

Your Father instructs you to turn away from the superficial, irreverent godless chatter that characterizes the conversations of people who are worldly-oriented. "Do not love or cherish the world or the things that are in the world. If anyone loves the world, love for the Father is not in him. For all that is in the world – the lust of the flesh [craving for sensual gratification] and the lust of the eyes [greedy longings of the mind] and the pride of life [assurance in one's own resources or in the stability of earthly things] – these do not come from the Father but are from the world [itself]." (I John 2:15-16 AMP)

God repeatedly tells you that you should not pursue worldly goals. These goals invariably focus on self-centeredness and selfish desires. God wants you to focus on His will for your life. He wants you to trust Him completely instead of trusting in your limited human abilities and worldly sources of security. "If then you have died with Christ to material ways of looking at things and have escaped from the world's crude and elemental notions and teachings of externalism, why do you live as if you still belong to the world?..." (Colossians 2:20 AMP)

You are instructed to die to the ways of the world. Some Christians who do their best to live good and moral lives still live as though they belong to the world. They do not understand and faithfully obey the scriptural instructions that we are studying in this chapter. Living this way blocks these Christians from hearing the voice of God.

Many Christians have no concept of the spiritual damage that is caused by what they allow to come into their eyes and their ears from television, movies, radio and other worldly methods of communication. They allow their eyes and their ears to be filled with concepts that are directly opposed to the teaching of God's Word.

Never before in the history of the world have there been so many voices clamoring for your attention. You must learn how to tune *out* the discordant things that come from the world so that you can tune *in* to the voice of God. As you saw in Chapter 3, Jesus has warned you to be careful about what you hear (see Mark 4:24).

The world today is much noisier than it was when your parents and grandparents were your age. Hearing God's voice is more difficult today than it was one or two generations ago. Focus consistently on turning *away* from everything in this noisy world that will distract you from hearing what God is saying to you.

In this age of the internet, people are becoming increasingly focused on the latest electronic gadgets instead of faithfully obeying God's instructions to study His Word each day and to meditate day and night on His Word. The lives of many people today revolve around their smart phones, text messaging, Facebook, Twitter, YouTube and other social media. "…set your minds and keep them set on what is above (the higher things), not on the things that are on the earth." (Colossians 3:2 AMP)

Please note that this verse instructs you to *keep* your mind set on the higher things of God. Do not allow the temporal things of the world to consume your thinking. "…come out from among [unbelievers], and separate (sever) yourselves from them…" (II Corinthians 6:17 AMP)

If you truly desire to hear God's voice, you must consistently *separate* yourself from the way that unbelievers live. Learn to live your life from the inside out, not from the outside in. Instead of basing your life primarily on what is happening in the world, you should turn away from worldly distractions to draw closer to God.

We are not saying that you should ignore everything in the world. You should keep up with what is happening in the world. Do not make the mistake of constantly being barraged by the outpouring of bad news from the news media. Meditate day and night on the good news of God's Word instead of focusing on the bad news that is so predominant in the world today.

Put God in first place where He belongs and keep Him first (see I Samuel 12:20-21, Matthew 6:33, John 3:30 and Colossians 1:8). Put your recreational activities and everything else that you do *after* your time with God. Do not put the God of the universe in last place and yourself, your personal desires and the things of the world ahead of God.

This chapter contains repeated instructions from the Bible to turn away from the world. You must obey these instructions from God if you sincerely desire to hear Him speaking to you.

Chapter 12

The Importance of Daily Quiet Time with God

In the last chapter we studied instructions from God that instructed you to turn away from the ways of the world. In this chapter we will study Scripture that will tell you *how* to turn away from the world. We will focus on Scripture that will explain God's instructions about setting aside quiet time each day to be alone with Him.

There is a definite relationship between daily quiet time with God and hearing God's voice. Jesus Christ is your example in every area of your life. The Bible explains the importance that Jesus placed on quiet time with His Father. "…the news spread abroad concerning Him, and great crowds kept coming together to hear [Him] and to be healed by Him of their infirmities. But He Himself withdrew [in retirement] to the wilderness (desert) and prayed." (Luke 5:15-16 AMP)

So many people were talking about the miraculous healings that people were experiencing from Jesus that a large crowd of people came to hear Him speak and to be healed. Jesus apparently knew that He was not ready to minister to these people. He turned away from them and their desire to be taught and to be healed. He went into the desert for a quiet time of prayer to His Father.

The Bible explains other instances that emphasize the quiet time that Jesus spent alone with His Father. Jesus did not allow anything, no matter how important it seemed, to take priority over His precious quiet time with God.

Jesus did not spend just a few minutes with God. He spent significant amounts of quiet time with God. "…it came to pass in those days, that he went out into a mountain to pray, and continued all night in prayer to God." (Luke 6:12 KJV)

This verse explains that Jesus spent the entire night in prayer. Emphasize the importance of your daily quiet time with God. No appointment on your daily appointment schedule can even remotely approach the importance of your daily time with God.

God explains what your priorities should be in the following passage of Scripture. "…Jesus entered a certain village, and a woman named Martha received and welcomed Him into her house. And she had a sister named Mary, who seated herself at the Lord's feet and was listening to His teaching. But Martha [overly occupied and too busy] was distracted with much serving; and she came up to Him and said, Lord, is it nothing to You that my sister has left me to serve alone? Tell her then to help me [to lend a hand and do her part along with me]! But the Lord replied to her by saying, Martha, Martha, you are anxious and troubled about many things; There is need of only one or but a few things. Mary has chosen the good portion [that which is to her advantage], which shall not be taken away from her.' (Luke 10:38-42 AMP)

Martha was *overly occupied and too busy* serving Jesus. Mary sat at His feet learning from Him. When Martha complained that Mary should be helping her, Jesus told her that Mary was doing what was important.

Many ladies are amused by this passage. When the time comes for the meal, if Martha spent all of her time with Jesus, there would be no meal. No one who is in charge of a household can spend all of her time in prayer and worshiping the Lord. We have to look at this verse in the spirit in which it was written. The work does have to be done. The clear message is that our service for the Lord can never replace our relationship with Him.

Many Christians make the mistake of doing what Martha did. They are so busily engaged in various activities that seem important to them that they do not set aside the precious quiet time with God that is vital to hearing God's voice. The Bible instructs you to "…pursue that consecration and holiness without which no one will [ever] see the Lord." (Hebrews 12:14 AMP)

When this verse speaks of pursuing consecration, it refers to setting aside time to seek holiness. You cannot experience holiness in the ways of the world. You can only experience holiness to the degree that you consistently spend time alone with God, turning away from worldly activities.

Joshua succeeded Moses as the leader of Israel. Joshua explained to the Israelites the importance of turning away from worldly activities. He said, "…Sanctify yourselves [that is, separate yourselves for a special holy purpose]…" (Joshua 3:5 AMP)

These words that Joshua spoke to the Israelites apply to your life today. You are instructed to sanctify yourself. The amplification explains that you sanctify yourself by separating yourself for a holy purpose.

Your daily quiet time with God is not an option. This time each day is a necessity. "…set your mind and heart to seek (inquire of and require as your vital necessity) the Lord your God…" (I Chronicles 22:19 AMP)

Please note the words "vital necessity" in the amplification of this verse. Seeking the Lord is an absolute *necessity*. Turn away from the fast-paced lifestyle of our generation. If you give quiet time with God the priority that it deserves, you will draw closer to God. You will hear Him speaking to you. The psalmist said, "…He leads me beside the still and restful waters. He refreshes and restores my life (my self)…" (Psalm 23:2-3 AMP)

The well-known 23rd Psalm speaks of "still and restful waters." If you are still and quiet before God each day, He will refresh you. He will restore you.

Once again, Jesus is your example in every area of your life. Throughout His earthly ministry Jesus turned away from what He was doing for precious quiet time with His Father. "And in the morning, long before daylight, He got up and went out to a deserted place, and there He prayed." (Mark 1:35 AMP)

Please note that this verse speaks specifically of Jesus getting His quality time with His Father early in the *morning*. The Bible consistently instructs you to set aside quiet time to be with God in the morning.

The early morning hours provide a great opportunity to set the foundation for the remainder of your day. The Bible says that God wants to spend time with you in the morning. "What is man that You should magnify him and think him important? And that You should set Your mind upon him? And that You should visit him every morning…" (Job 7:17-18 AMP)

Your morning quiet time is very important to God. He wants to visit you *every* morning. The psalmist David knew the importance of spending quality time with God in the morning. He said, "In the morning You hear my voice, O Lord; in the morning I prepare [a prayer, a sacrifice] for You and watch and wait [for You to speak to my heart]." (Psalm 5:3 AMP)

Please note that this verse explains the relationship between consistent quiet time with the Lord in the morning and *hearing* God speak to your heart. At a later time David said, "Cause me to hear Your loving-kindness in the morning, for on You do I lean and in You do I trust. Cause me to know the way wherein I should walk, for I lift up my inner self to You." (Psalm 143:8 AMP)

Once again you see the relationship between quiet time with God in the morning and *hearing* Him speaking to you. God will guide you throughout each day if you lift up your inner self to Him each morning.

Why would any mature Christian ever allow a business appointment, a social event or a recreational activity to come ahead of the privilege of spending time alone with God? How can appointments with men and women who were created by God take precedence over the unique opportunity to spend quality time with the same God Who created every person on earth?

What should you do in your daily quiet time with God each morning? Every person is different. We recommend that you spend part of this time in prayer, part of this time in praise and worship, part of this time in Bible study and Scripture meditation and part of this time just being quiet before God. The psalmist indicated that he spent time meditating on God's Word early in the morning. He said, "…I am awake before the cry of the watchman, that I may meditate on Your word." (Psalm 119:148 AMP)

There were no alarm clocks when this verse was written. The watchman in each town awakened the townspeople early in the morning with a loud cry. The psalmist arose very early in the morning so that he could meditate on God's Word.

If you are a busy and active person and you are not used to having quiet time in your life, you should expect the time that you set aside to be with God to be difficult at first. Some people find that their minds are filled with distracting thoughts. Other people find that this early morning time alone with God is drudgery because it is so different from anything they have ever done.

Do not give up. If you persevere in setting aside quiet time to be alone with God each morning, you ultimately will look forward with great anticipation to this precious time each day. You will cherish your quiet time with God. You will not miss this time for anything.

You can have wonderful time with God in addition to the quiet time that you spend with Him each morning. I have walked at least 6 days a week for many years. I used to walk 60 minutes a day. Then I walked 45 minutes a day. Now that I am 81 years old, I walk approximately 30 minutes a day. All of my walking time is quiet time with God. I pray during this precious quiet time when I walk. I sing praise and I worship God.

Also, I never get into my car when I am driving alone without having worship music playing automatically as soon as I turn on the ignition. I have many hours of recorded worship music in my car. I consistently praise God and thank Him when I am driving my car.

If you develop a habit of setting aside quiet time with God over a period of months and years, your sensitivity to God will increase. You not only will hear God speaking to you when you are quiet, but you also will be able to hear His voice in the midst of a crowd of people and at other times when you are surrounded by noise.

Some people initially find that setting aside this quiet time each day causes them to be lonely. If you have this problem, Jesus gave you the answer when He said, "…I am not alone, because the Father is with Me." (John 16:32 AMP)

Jesus was always conscious of His Father's presence. As you develop this quiet time with God each day, you will be more and more conscious of God's indwelling presence. Once you establish an intimate relationship with God, you will never be lonely.

Chapter 13

You Hear the Voice of God within Yourself

When you think about hearing the voice of God, you must realize that you are not listening to a voice that is far above the earth in heaven. "Am I a God at hand, says the Lord, and not a God afar off?" (Jeremiah 23:23 AMP)

God says that He is not far away from you. You are not listening to God speaking to you from His throne in heaven. If you will carefully study and meditate on the Scripture references in this chapter, you will clearly see that God lives *inside* of you. When you hear God's voice, you usually hear Him speaking within yourself.

We now would like to look again at a verse of Scripture that we studied in Chapter 1. The same mighty God Who created heaven and earth lives in *your* heart if Jesus Christ is your Savior. "One God and Father of [us] all, Who is above all [Sovereign over all], pervading all and [living] in [us] all." (Ephesians 4:6 AMP)

We explained in Chapter 1 that God is omnipresent. He could not be closer to you. He lives in your heart and in the heart of every other person who has received Jesus Christ as his or her Savior. "The Lord your God is in the midst of you, a Mighty One…" (Zephaniah 3:17 AMP)

If you understand that Almighty God lives inside of you and that He is speaking to you from within your heart, you will have a much better foundation to learn how to hear His voice. God has placed everything that you will ever need inside of you. Jesus said, "...the kingdom of God is within you [in your hearts]..." (Luke 17:21 AMP)

God does not speak to you through the ears that you have on each side of your head. God gave you these ears to hear things in the world. The ears that you hear God speaking to you with are your spiritual ears.

You have within yourself a distinct and separate spiritual person who is different from the outer you that other people see when they look at you. The Bible refers to this person as "...the hidden person of the heart, with the incorruptible and unfading charm of a gentle and peaceful spirit, which [is not anxious or wrought up, but] is very precious in the sight of God.." (I Peter 3:4 AMP)

The outer person that the world looks at when they see you is not the real you. The real you is the hidden person of the heart. This verse explains that the hidden person of the heart is gentle and peaceful. He is never anxious or worried. The hidden person of the heart is very precious in the sight of God.

You can only understand hearing the voice of God to the degree that you comprehend that God is speaking from within you to a spiritual person who also lives within you. The hidden person of the heart who lives deep down inside of you hears everything that God says. You must learn how to tune in to God within you and the hidden person within you.

When your life is based on a constant awareness of God living in your heart and the hidden person living in your heart, you then will see life from God's perspective. You will be able to hear God's voice clearly.

Jesus Christ was continually conscious of God's indwelling presence throughout His earthly ministry. He heard God speaking to Him within Himself. He knew that the great miracles that He performed came from within Him. Jesus said, "...the Father Who lives continually in Me does the (His) works (His own miracles, deeds of power)." (John 14:10 AMP)

You should have a constant awareness of the indwelling presence of God. Wherever you go, God goes with you. God said, "...I am with you and will keep (watch over you with care, take notice of) you wherever you may go..." (Genesis 28:15 AMP)

You can be certain that God is with you at all times. He is watching over you. He never leaves you. When Joshua succeeded Moses as the leader of Israel, God assured Joshua that He was with him at all times. God said, "...As I was with Moses, so I will be with you; I will not fail you or forsake you." (Joshua 1:5 AMP)

God spoke these words to Joshua to assure him that He would be with him at all times and that He would never let him down. The same promise that God made to Joshua many years ago applies to your life today.

All that God asks is for you to meditate consistently on these passages of Scripture pertaining to His indwelling presence. Your Father wants you to have absolute faith that He is with you, that He is watching over you and that He will never fail you. "Have not I commanded you? Be strong, vigorous, and very courageous. Be not afraid, neither be dismayed, for the Lord your God is with you wherever you go." (Joshua 1:9 AMP)

God continued to speak to Joshua, assuring him that He was with him. God *commanded* Joshua to be strong and courageous because he trusted Him. God told Joshua that he should not be afraid because He was with him at all times.

This same command applies to you. Know that God lives within you. Trust Him completely. Every aspect of your life should revolve around your absolute certainty that Almighty God *does* live in your heart. "...in Him we live and move and have our being..." (Acts 17:28 AMP)

If Jesus Christ is your Savior, you are a spiritual powerhouse. You have seen that God lives in your heart. Jesus Christ also makes

His permanent home in your heart. "May Christ through your faith [actually] dwell (settle down, abide, make His permanent home) in your hearts!..." (Ephesians 3:17 AMP)

God lives in your heart. Jesus lives in your heart. The Holy Spirit also lives in your heart. "…God's Spirit has His permanent dwelling in you [to be at home in you, collectively as a church and also individually]…" (I Corinthians 3:16 AMP)

There is no question that you have the supernatural power of God, Jesus Christ and the Holy Spirit within you. "…you are in Him, made full and having come to fullness of life [in Christ you too are filled with the Godhead—Father, Son and Holy Spirit—and reach full spiritual stature]…." (Colossians 2:10 AMP)

Turn *away* from the world. There is nothing of eternal significance in the world. Everything in the world is temporary and superficial. Turn continually toward God Who lives within you. The more that you are conscious of God's indwelling presence and the more your life revolves around your absolute certainty that God lives within you, the more clearly you will hear His voice.

Chapter 14

The Voice of God and the Voice of Satan

Now that you have learned that the voice of God comes from within you, we are ready to look into the Bible for more information pertaining to the voice of God. We will begin by studying Scripture that says that God has spoken in a very loud voice. "Hear, oh, hear the roar of His voice and the sound of rumbling that goes out of His mouth! Under the whole heaven He lets it loose, and His lightning to the ends of the earth. After it His voice roars; He thunders with the voice of His majesty…" (Job 37:2-4 AMP)

This passage of Scripture compares God's majestic voice to thunder. On one occasion when Jesus was speaking to a group of people, God spoke loudly to these people. "The crowd of bystanders heard the sound and said that it had thundered; others said, An angel has spoken to Him!" (John 12:29 AMP)

Once again, God's voice is compared to thunder. God has enormous supernatural power. His voice has great power. When God chooses to speak loudly, He can speak very loudly. "…His voice was like the sound of many waters…" (Ezekiel 43:2 AMP)

Usually when God speaks in a loud voice, He speaks to a large group of people. When God speaks to you individually, He very seldom, if ever, will speak in a loud voice. Even though God's voice has great power, He invariably speaks softly and gently to

His children. The prophet Elijah said that God's voice is "…[a sound of gentle stillness and] a still, small voice." (I Kings 19:12 AMP)

You have seen that God speaks from within you to the hidden person who lives in your heart. There is no need for God to speak loudly when He is speaking from deep down inside of you to the hidden person in your heart.

God speaks to His children in a still, small voice because He wants each of us to have great sensitivity to His voice. As you become more and more conscious of God's indwelling presence and your life revolves around your absolute certainty that God lives in your heart, you will hear His still, small voice more clearly.

In Chapter 7 we studied Scripture pertaining to a close and intimate relationship with God. If you have an intimate relationship with God, you will be calm, quiet and trusting within yourself, regardless of external circumstances. You will have great sensitivity to God and His voice. In this tranquil atmosphere you always will be able to hear God speaking softly to you. Your spiritual growth and maturity will assure you that you are hearing from God.

God will speak audibly when He wants to be absolutely certain that you hear what He is saying. Hearing the audible voice of God is very rare. Many mature Christians go through their entire lives without hearing the audible voice of God one time.

I have only heard God speak to me audibly one time in the 38 years that I have been a Christian. When I moved to Florida 25 years ago, I rented an apartment. Once I was situated, I began to look for a house. I was not certain where God wanted me to live.

One night I was driving in the dark on a road about 45 minutes north of where I lived. I was driving to teach at a home fellowship group from our church. As I was driving along in the dark I suddenly heard God say audibly, "*This* is where I want you to live."

I looked to my left and I saw a sign with the name of a housing development. When I arrived at the home fellowship group, I asked the people who lived in this area where this housing development was located. They told me that it was located in Dunedin.

The next morning I opened the classified advertising section of the newspaper to the real estate section. I turned to Dunedin. The first listing was a description of exactly the kind of home I was looking for. I called and made an appointment to see this house. When I drove into the driveway, I had a deep inner certainty that this was the home that God had for me. I had never experienced anything like that before.

When I rang the doorbell and the door was opened, the first thing I saw was a Christian plaque on the wall just inside the front door. As the owners showed me the house, I was even more certain that this was the house where God wanted me to live.

After a thorough inspection, I sat with the owners at a table on the patio. We prayed together seeking God's will for my life in regard to a home. Everything fell into place. There was no doubt then and there has been no doubt since then that this is the home where God wants me to live. I have lived in this home for 23 years. God is the greatest Realtor in the universe.

I cherish the one time that I clearly heard God speaking audibly to me, telling me exactly where He wanted me to live. God cares about every minute detail of the lives of His beloved children. I am so grateful that He spoke audibly to me to make absolutely certain that I knew where He wanted me to live. Judy and I were married shortly after that. She shares my conviction that this is the home that God has for us.

Now that we have looked into the Word of God at Scripture pertaining to God's voice, we are ready to look into God's Word for Scripture pertaining to the other spiritual voice that people hear – the voice of Satan. Numerous surveys have indicated that a significant percentage of Christians do not believe that Satan exists or that his demons can speak to them. This is *exactly* what Satan wants Christians to believe.

The Bible teaches that Satan originally was an archangel named Lucifer who was so proud that he wanted to be like God (see Isaiah 14:12-17). Satan was supported by many fallen angels. Satan and his fallen angels were cast out of heaven because of their pride (see Ezekiel 28:17 and Revelation 12:9).

The atmosphere around the world today is filled with God's angels and with Satan's proud fallen angels who are called demons. There is no question that Satan's demons can speak to people.

We have explained that God is omnipresent. He can be in an infinite number of places at the same time. You have seen that God can speak to billions of people throughout the world at the same time. Satan is not omnipresent. He can only be in one place at a time. Satan has to depend on his demons to speak to people individually.

Satan's demons in the atmosphere around you observe you carefully. They do everything they can to influence unbelievers not to receive Jesus Christ as their Savior. If Jesus is your Savior, Satan's demons will do everything they can to stop you from serving Jesus and living the way that God instructs you to live. They do *not* want you to hear God's voice.

Satan's demons can possess unbelievers, but they cannot possess a Christian. The Holy Spirit lives inside of every person who has received Jesus Christ as his or her Savior. Satan and his demons cannot possess Christians who have the Holy Spirit living within them. However, Satan's demons can oppress Christians.

Some Christians never hear God's voice throughout their lives. Other Christians only hear God's voice occasionally. Many Christians hear the voice of Satan's demons often.

Satan always is exactly the opposite of God. God is gentle and loving. He will never force Himself on you. You can only hear His still, small voice to the degree that you are quiet enough within yourself to hear Him speaking to the hidden person of your heart.

Satan's demons are just the opposite. They hate all Christians. They will try to force themselves on you in any way that they can. They are very insistent. They also are clever and subtle. They are deceivers. They will try to deceive you in any way they can. You do not need to learn how to hear the voices of Satan's demons. They speak daily to billions of people all over the world.

Satan spoke to Eve in the garden of Eden, trying to influence her to disobey God (see Genesis 3:1-6). The New Testament talks of Satan speaking to people when he spoke to Jesus. "Then Jesus was led (guided) by the [Holy] Spirit into the wilderness (desert) to be tempted (tested and tried) by the devil. And He went without food for forty days and forty nights, and later He was hungry." (Matthew 4:1-2 AMP)

The Holy Spirit actually led Jesus into the desert to be tempted, tested and tried by the devil. Before Jesus could begin His earthly ministry, He had to go for 40 days and 40 nights without food. Jesus was very hungry at the end of this fast. Satan spoke to Jesus. "And the tempter came and said to Him, If You are God's Son, command these stones to be made [loaves of] bread." (Matthew 4:3 AMP)

Satan told Jesus that, if He really was the Son of God, He should be able to turn stones into bread to satisfy His hunger. Jesus said, "…It has been written, Man shall not live and be upheld and sustained by bread alone, but by every word that comes forth from the mouth of God." (Matthew 4:4 AMP)

Matthew 4:5-6 gives another example of Satan speaking to Jesus. Matthew 4:8-9 gives another example of Satan speaking to Jesus. There is no question that Satan was able to speak to Jesus as he attempted to influence Him in the wilderness before He began His earthly ministry.

We see another example of Satan speaking to an individual when he spoke to Judas Iscariot who was a disciple of Jesus. Satan's goal was to persuade Judas to betray Jesus. "So [it was] during supper, Satan having already put the thought of betraying Jesus in the heart of Judas Iscariot, Simon's son." (John 13:2 AMP)

Even though Judas actually was the treasurer of the disciples (see John 12:6 and 13:29), Satan was able to persuade him to betray Jesus. Judas subsequently betrayed Jesus by leading a group of angry people to arrest Him (see Matthew 26:45-50).

You have just seen that Satan definitely spoke to Jesus and to Judas Iscariot. Satan and his demons have not changed. They have not gone anywhere. Satan's demons still speak to people today just as Satan spoke to Jesus and to Judas in the Scripture you have just read.

If you choose to believe that Satan's demons do not exist and that they cannot speak to you, you make their job much easier. The Bible teaches that Satan has significant influence in the world (see I Corinthians 4:4 and I John 5:19). You saw in Chapter 11 that the Bible teaches you to consistently turn away from the world.

You cannot hear God's voice if your life revolves primarily around things in the world. Whenever Satan's demons speak to you, whatever they are saying will not line up with the Truth of the Word of God. Jesus, speaking of Satan, said, "…there is no truth in him. When he speaks a falsehood, he speaks what is natural to him, for he is a liar [himself] and the father of lies and of all that is false." (John 8:44 AMP)

This verse explains that all lies in the world are influenced by Satan. You saw in Chapter 9 that you will block yourself from hearing God's voice if you disobey God's instructions to study His Word each day and to meditate day and night on the holy Scriptures. "…the Word of God is [always] abiding in you (in your hearts), and you have been victorious over the wicked one." (I John 2:14 AMP)

You cannot resist Satan's demons with human willpower. The only way that you can resist what Satan's demons are saying to you or to resist Satan's demons in any other way is to the degree that your heart is filled with the Word of God (see James 4:7 and I Peter 5:6-9).

If you have paid the price of studying God's Word and meditating day and night on the holy Scriptures, you will place yourself in a spiritual position where you can hear God's voice and where you also will be able to identify the voice of Satan. You will be like the psalmist David who said, "…by the word of Your lips I have avoided the ways of the violent (the paths of the destroyer)." (Psalm 17:4 AMP)

When the amplification speaks of the destroyer, this word refers to Satan and his demons. Jesus said, "The thief comes only in order to steal and kill and destroy…." (John 10:10 AMP)

In this chapter we have studied scriptural truths pertaining to the voice of God and the voice of Satan. In the next chapter we will study several passages of Scripture that will explain how many people block themselves from hearing the voice of God and open themselves to hear the voice of Satan's demons.

Chapter 15

Do Not Block Yourself from Hearing God's Voice

God wants very much for every one of His children to hear His voice just as He wanted the Israelites in the wilderness to hear His voice. God said, "…My people would not hearken to My voice, and Israel would have none of Me. So I gave them up to their own hearts' lust and let them go after their own stubborn will, that they might follow their own counsels." (Psalm 81:11-12 AMP)

God wanted the Israelites to hear what He was saying to them, but they refused to listen. God had no alternative except to allow them to do whatever they wanted to do. Anyone who has consistently studied the Bible knows that the Israelites repeatedly got themselves into trouble by doing what seemed right to them instead of doing what God instructed them to do.

This same principle applies to Christians today. If Jesus Christ is your Savior, you have been given the ability to hear God speaking to you throughout every day of your life. Do not block God as the Israelites did.

Your Father loves you. He wants you to take full advantage of the ability He has given you to hear what He is saying to you. He wants you to obey His instructions. "…see to it that you do not reject Him or refuse to listen to and heed Him Who is speaking [to you now]…" (Hebrews 12:25 AMP)

In the first 14 chapters of this book we have given you many verses of Scripture explaining that God speaks continually to His children. Do not block yourself from hearing what God is saying by failing to learn how to hear His voice.

Some Christians block themselves from hearing the voice of God because they are busily engaged in doing what they think is important instead of learning how to hear God's voice and obeying God's instructions. You will not hear what God is saying to you if you do what seems right to you instead of doing what God instructs you to do. "There is a way which seems right to a man and appears straight before him, but at the end of it is the way of death." (Proverbs 14:12 AMP)

Many people are spiritually dead because they do what seems right to them instead of learning how to hear what God says and obeying His instructions. If you sincerely desire to hear God's voice, you must turn away from the limitations of human logic and intellectual worldly thinking. "…this world's wisdom is foolishness (absurdity and stupidity) with God…" (I Corinthians 3:19 AMP)

God looks at the wisdom of the world as being "foolish, absurd and stupid." You will make the same mistake that the Israelites made if you do what seems right to you based upon a worldly perspective instead of learning how to hear God's voice and doing what He instructs you to do. The Bible goes on to say "…The Lord knows the thoughts and reasonings of the [humanly] wise and recognizes how futile they are." (I Corinthians 3:20 AMP)

Traditional worldly thinking says that you cannot hear God talking to *you* individually throughout every day of your life. You have seen that the Word of God says otherwise. Jesus told a group of Pharisees, "…You have a fine way of rejecting [thus thwarting and nullifying and doing away with] the commandment of God in order to keep your tradition (your own human regulations)!" (Mark 7:9 AMP)

The Pharisees turned away from God's instructions. They did what made sense to their traditional thinking. Jesus later told the Pharisees, "…you are nullifying and making void and of no effect [the authority of] the Word of God through your tradition, which you [in turn] hand on…." (Mark 7:13 AMP)

You learned in Chapter 8 that the Word of God is spiritually alive and filled with the supernatural power of God (see Hebrews 4:12). Nevertheless, you *are* able to block the supernatural power of God's Word in regard to hearing God's voice if you think traditionally instead of learning and obeying God's instructions to hear His voice.

Religious tradition blocks many Christians from hearing God's voice. The concept of God speaking individually to every person who has received Jesus Christ as his or her Savior is completely foreign to Christians who have not carefully studied this topic in the Word of God. Turn away from traditional thinking that has been handed down from generation to generation. Be determined that you *will* hear God's voice by learning and obeying God's specific instructions in this area.

If you insist on doing what seems right to you instead of being humble and teachable, you are proud because you insist on doing what you think is right. Pride always keeps people away from God. Proud people actually are their own little gods. They pay no attention to God's specific instructions. They do what they want to do.

Proud people are influenced by Satan's demons. You saw in the last chapter that Satan and his demons were cast out of heaven because of their pride, so you can be certain that Satan and his demons are proud. Satan's demons will try to influence these people to make the same mistake that they made. "…God sets Himself against the proud (the insolent, the overbearing, the disdainful, the presumptuous, the boastful) – [and He opposes, frustrates, and defeats them], but gives grace (favor, blessing) to the humble." (I Peter 5:5 AMP)

This verse shows you *how much* God dislikes pride. God loves every person on earth unconditionally, but if you are proud and you do things your way instead of learning and obeying God's instructions, you will cause your Father to set Himself against you.

The amplification of this verse says that God will "oppose, frustrate and defeat" people who are proud. No one wants Almighty God opposing them, frustrating them and defeating them, but this is exactly what happens to proud people. You must humble yourself before God. You must be willing to pay the price to learn God's specific instructions to hear His voice.

Proud people have hard hearts. They do what they think they should do instead of having a humble and teachable heart that yearns to do exactly what God says. "Blessed (happy, fortunate, and to be envied) is the man who reverently and worshipfully fears [the Lord] at all times [regardless of circumstances], but he who hardens his heart will fall into calamity." (Proverbs 28:14 AMP)

God will bless His children whose words and actions show that they truly fear Him and revere Him, regardless of the circumstance they face. If you have a hard heart, you will not learn and obey God's instructions. This attitude always will bring adversity into your life.

You saw in the beginning of this chapter how the Israelites blocked themselves from hearing God's voice. If you have a hard heart and you live your life your way instead of learning and obeying God's specific instructions, you also will block yourself from hearing His voice. "…Today, if you will hear His voice, Do not harden your hearts, as [happened] in the rebellion [of Israel] and their provocation and embitterment [of Me] in the day of testing in the wilderness" (Hebrews 3:7-8 AMP)

In the next chapter of the Book of Hebrews, God made a similar statement. He said, "…Today, if you would hear His voice and when you hear it, do not harden your hearts." (Hebrews 4:7 AMP)

In this chapter you have learned that you can block yourself from hearing the voice of God through worldly logic and intellectual thinking, through traditional beliefs that are handed down from one generation to another and through pride that leads to a hard heart. In the next chapter we will look into the Word of God for additional specific instructions that will tell you exactly what your Father instructs you to do to hear His voice.

Chapter 16

Humble Yourself and Keep God in First Place

You saw in the last chapter that God resists people who are proud and that pride will block you from hearing the voice of God. If you truly are humble, you will be much more likely to hear God speaking to you. "…though the Lord is high, yet has He respect to the lowly [bringing them into fellowship with Him]…" (Psalm 138:6 AMP)

God always resists pride. He always honors humility. You did not earn the right to hear God's voice. You do not deserve this privilege. "…He gives His undeserved favor to the low [in rank], the humble, and the afflicted." (Proverbs 3:34 AMP)

The words "undeserved favor" refer to the grace of God. God is gracious to His humble children. "…knowledge is easy to him who [being teachable] understands." (Proverbs 14:6 AMP)

Christians who truly are humble always are teachable. They sincerely desire to learn what God teaches. God wants to teach you and to guide you throughout every day of your life. "He leads the humble in what is right, and the humble He teaches His way." (Psalm 25:9 AMP)

God will lead you and guide you if you are humble. He will teach you how He wants you to live. If you truly are humble, you will obey God's instructions to pray consistently (see I Thessalonians 5:17). God is delighted when you come to Him in prayer asking Him to speak to you. "...the prayer of the upright is His delight!" (Proverbs 15:8 AMP)

In Chapter 7 we studied several Scripture references that explain the relationship between an intimate relationship with God and hearing His voice. In Chapters 8 and 9 we studied the relationship between consistently filling your mind and your heart with God's Word and hearing God's voice. God will answer your prayers to hear His voice if you are close to Him and if your mind and your heart are filled with His Word. Jesus said, "If you live in Me [abide vitally united to Me] and My words remain in you and continue to live in your hearts, ask whatever you will, and it shall be done for you." (John 15:7 AMP)

The amplification of this verse explains the vital importance of abiding in Jesus. When you abide in Jesus, you stay close to Him at all times. Jesus says that His Word should "remain in you and continue to live in your heart."

If you truly desire to hear God speaking to you, God must be in first place in your life. The intimacy of your relationship with Him should be very important to you. Anything that consistently occupies your attention ahead of God actually is your god. God said, "You shall have no other gods before or besides Me." (Exodus 20:3 AMP)

In this book we are speaking specifically of hearing God's voice. Do not allow the pursuit of pleasure, the desire for wealth or any other desire to come ahead of your desire to draw closer to God and to hear His voice. Jesus said, "...seek (aim at and strive after) first of all His kingdom and His righteousness (His way of doing and being right), and then all these things taken together will be given you besides." (Matthew 6:33 AMP)

If you truly keep God in first place at all times, He promises to meet all of your needs. This promise includes hearing His voice. As you grow and mature spiritually Jesus, in addition to being your Savior, should be the Lord of every day of your life.

Is Jesus more important to you than He was a month ago, three months ago, and one year ago? Are you obeying the following instruction from John the Baptist who said, "He must increase, but I must decrease. [He must grow more prominent; I must grow less so.]?" (John 3:30 AMP)

Jesus should always come ahead of your personal goals and desires. There is no question that there is a definite relationship between keeping Jesus in first place in your life and hearing God's voice.

Jesus rose from the dead so that you can live eternally in heaven. Every aspect of your life should revolve around Him. "He also is the Head of [His] body, the church; seeing He is the Beginning, the Firstborn from among the dead, so that He alone in everything and in every respect might occupy the chief place [stand first and be preeminent]." (Colossians 1:18 AMP)

This verse says that Jesus should be first "in everything and in every respect." If you truly keep God in first place and yearn to hear His voice, God will honor this desire. "…if from there you will seek (inquire for and require as necessity) the Lord your God, you will find Him if you [truly] seek Him with all your heart [and mind] and soul and life." (Deuteronomy 4:29 AMP)

Is keeping God first an absolute necessity in your life? Do you seek Him with all your heart and mind and soul? God speaks to His children who truly keep Him in first place at all times. You *will* find God and hear His voice if you continually seek Him with all your heart.

The best place that you can be in the spiritual realm is to be in last place because you have put God in first place in every aspect of your life. God deserves to be in first place. Refuse to allow anyone or anything to come ahead of God. "…not going your own way or seeking or finding your own pleasure or speaking with your own [idle] words, then will you delight yourself in the Lord, and I will make you to ride on the high places of the earth" (Isaiah 58:13-14 AMP)

You will not hear God speaking to you if you consistently go your own way. God will lift you up and you will hear His voice if you *delight* in Him and if every area of your life revolves around your continual consciousness of His indwelling presence.

You are living the way that God wants you to live if you gladly give up your God-given right to control of your life to allow the Holy Spirit to control your life. "…you are living the life of the Spirit, if the [Holy] Spirit of God [really] dwells within you [directs and controls you]…" (Romans 8:9 AMP)

Get out of the driver's seat. Allow the Holy Spirit to control your life. "…walk and live [habitually] in the [Holy] Spirit [responsive to and controlled and guided by the Spirit]; then you will certainly not gratify the cravings and desires of the flesh (of human nature without God)." (Galatians 5:16 AMP)

Please note that the amplification of this verse instructs you to live your life with the Holy Spirit in control, not yourself. If the Holy Spirit truly is in control, you will not pursue carnal desires. You will be close to God and you will continually hear Him speaking to you.

In this chapter we have studied several verses of Scripture that explain the relationship between hearing God's voice and humility, praying consistently, keeping God first and yielding control of your life to the Holy Spirit. In the next chapter we will study additional instructions from God that will enable you to hear Him speaking to you.

Chapter 17

Fear God and Focus on Him

In the last two chapters we essentially profiled the lifestyle of a Christian who is able to hear God's voice. In this chapter we will continue this study by looking at what the Bible says about the relationship between fearing God and consistently hearing His voice.

First we will explain what fearing God is. Fear usually is looked at as something that is negative. Fearing God is completely positive. If you truly fear God, you revere Him. You hold Him in constant awe. Your life revolves around Him.

Any person who is described by the words in the last three sentences *will* create a spiritual atmosphere that is conducive to hearing God's voice. "…the end of the matter is: Fear God [revere and worship Him, knowing that He is] and keep His commandments, for this is the whole of man [the full, original purpose of his creation, the object of God's providence, the root of character, the foundation of all happiness, the adjustment to all inharmonious circumstances and conditions under the sun] and the whole [duty] for every man." (Ecclesiastes 12:13 AMP)

Do you want to do exactly what God created you to do? God created you to fear Him, revere Him and worship Him. He created you to obey His instructions. These vitally important characteristics are the root of good character and "the foundation of *all* happiness." These characteristics will enable you to cope with and adjust to anything and everything that happens in your life. Living this way is the *duty* of every Christian. "Let all the earth fear the Lord [revere and worship Him]; let all the inhabitants of the world stand in awe of Him." (Psalm 33:8 AMP)

God instructs *every* person on earth to fear Him, revere Him and worship Him. If you are in complete awe of God, you will revere Him at all times. You will worship Him continually. "Blessed (happy, fortunate, to be envied) is everyone who fears, reveres, and worships the Lord, who walks in His ways and lives according to His commandments." (Psalm 128:1 AMP)

God promises to bless *every* person who fears Him, reveres Him, worships Him and obeys His instructions. This blessing includes hearing His voice. Your Father tells you exactly what to do to receive His blessings. "The secret [of the sweet, satisfying companionship] of the Lord have they who fear (revere and worship) Him, and He will show them His covenant and reveal to them its [deep, inner] meaning." (Psalm 25:14 AMP)

This verse and the amplification explain "the secret of a satisfying companionship of the Lord." If you truly fear God, He will reveal to you everything that He wants you to know. This includes hearing His voice. "You who [reverently] fear the Lord, trust in and lean on the Lord! He is their Help and their Shield." (Psalm 115:11 AMP)

If you truly fear God and revere Him, you will trust Him completely. If you fear God and trust Him, He will help you. He will protect you. One of the ways that God will help you is to enable you to hear what He continually is saying to you. "Who is the man who reverently fears and worships the Lord? Him shall He teach in the way that he should choose." (Psalm 25:12 AMP)

If you truly fear God, you will hear Him teaching you and showing you the way that He wants you to go. "The reverent, worshipful fear of the Lord leads to life, and he who has it rests satisfied; he cannot be visited with [actual] evil." (Proverbs 19:23 AMP)

You learned in Chapter 14 that Satan's demons often speak to people. If you truly fear God, Satan's demons will not be able to influence you by what they are saying to you. "…continue in the reverent and worshipful fear of the Lord all the day long." (Proverbs 23:17 AMP)

Do you want to hear God speaking to you throughout every day of your life? If you do, your lifestyle should be a lifestyle of consistently fearing God, revering Him, and worshiping Him.

If you truly fear God and revere Him, you will focus on Him continually. You will not allow anything to distract you from putting God in first place in your life and keeping Him there. You will be like the psalmist who said, "My eyes are ever toward the Lord..." (Psalm 25:15 AMP)

You should put God first and keep Him first at all times. "…[earnestly] remember the Lord and imprint Him [on your minds]…" (Nehemiah 4:14 AMP)

This verse and the amplification instruct you to "earnestly remember" the Lord. When you do something earnestly, you are diligent and persistent about whatever you are doing. You are instructed to *imprint* God on your mind. Every aspect of your life should revolve around the intimacy of your relationship with God.

If you face a seemingly severe problem, absolutely refuse to focus on whatever problem you face. You should be like Moses was when he approached the Red Sea with a very powerful Egyptian army behind him, impassable mountains to his right and left and the deep Red Sea ahead of him. "…he never flinched but held staunchly to his purpose and endured steadfastly as one who gazed on Him Who is invisible." (Hebrews 11:27 AMP)

Moses absolutely *refused* to focus on the seemingly overwhelming problems he faced. He focused on God. Moses did not give up because he continually "gazed on Him Who is invisible."

God honored the single-minded focus of Moses. God parted the waves of the Red Sea so that Moses and the Israelites could pass safely through. When Pharaoh and his army came, the water in the Red Sea returned to destroy them (see Exodus 14).

You should be like Moses. Some Christians go to church once or twice a week and spend a few minutes in routine prayer each day, but the rest of their lives are focused on themselves, their families, their vocation and different things in the world. Your Father wants *every* aspect of your life to revolve around Him. Do not allow anyone or anything to come ahead of God.

This chapter contains 11 passages of Scripture instructing you to fear God, to focus on God and to always keep God first in your life. This attitude is absolutely essential to hearing God speaking to you continually. In the next chapter you will learn how to actually come into the presence of God where you always will hear Him speaking to you.

Chapter 18

Praise God and Thank Him Continually

Christians who frequently grumble, gripe and complain block themselves from hearing God's voice. Your Father does not want you to complain. "Do all things without grumbling and faultfinding and complaining [against God]…" (Philippians 2:14 AMP).

Please note the words "all things" in this verse. If you complain, you actually are complaining against God. He will cause everything to ultimately work out for the best if you trust Him continually (see Romans 8:28).

Christians whose hearts are filled with gratitude to God will thank Him and praise Him continually. Deep and continual gratitude in your heart will open your spiritual ears to hear what God is saying to you.

You should be *so* grateful to God that you thank Him continually. Giving thanks to God should be a way of life to you. "At all times and for everything giving thanks in the name of our Lord Jesus Christ to God the Father." (Ephesians 5:20 AMP)

You are instructed to thank God "at *all* times and for *everything*." If what is happening does not seem to be good, thank God in the name of Jesus Christ for His many promises to bring you safely through whatever ordeal you face as you trust in Him (see Deuteronomy 28:13, Proverbs 18:14, Isaiah 43:2-3, Romans 8:37, II Corinthians 2:14 and I John 5:4).

Whenever God tells you the same thing two or more times, He is emphasizing what He is saying. "Thank [God] in everything [no matter what the circumstances may be, be thankful and give thanks], for this is the will of God for you [who are] in Christ Jesus [the Revealer and Mediator of that will]." (I Thessalonians 5:18 AMP)

Place all of your trust in God. He is in complete control. Thank God continually for causing everything to work out for the best. Praise Him and thank Him regardless of what is happening to you. "…let us offer the sacrifice of praise to God continually, that is, the fruit of our lips giving thanks to his name." (Hebrews 13:15 KJV)

You make a spiritual *sacrifice* when you praise God continually and thank Him continually, regardless of the circumstances that you face. If you praise God and thank Him at all times, you are not allowing the circumstances in your life to dictate what comes out of your mouth. God said, "He who brings an offering of praise and thanksgiving honors and glorifies Me…" (Psalm 50:23 AMP)

In Hebrews 13:15, praise was referred to as a sacrifice. Praise is referred to here as an offering. When you praise God and thank Him continually, you bring a spiritual offering to Him. You honor God and glorify Him if you praise Him and thank Him at all times. God said, "The people I formed for Myself, that they may set forth My praise.." (Isaiah 43:21 AMP)

This verse explains that God created you to praise Him. You saw in the last chapter that God created you to fear Him. Your Father wants your attitude toward Him to be a continual attitude of reverence and awe. He wants you to praise Him and thank Him continually. If the last two sentences describe your lifestyle, you *are* living the way that God created you to live.

Christians who praise God and thank Him repeatedly will hear His voice much more clearly and much more often than a person who does not consistently praise God and thank Him. Your absolute awe of God should be reflected by praise and thanksgiving constantly flowing out of your mouth. "Great is the Lord and highly to be praised..." (Psalm 145:3 AMP)

God is so great that our human vocabulary cannot even begin to describe the magnitude of His majesty. If you can even begin to comprehend how awesome and magnificent God is, you *will* praise Him and thank Him continually. "You are worthy, our Lord and God, to receive glory and honor and power, for you created all things, and by your will they were created and have their being" (Revelation 4:11 NIV)

God is worthy to receive your constant praise and thanksgiving. God created you. He created everything in the entire universe. "From the rising of the sun to the going down of it and from east to west, the name of the Lord is to be praised!" (Psalm 113:3 AMP)

You are instructed to praise God throughout the day and night. You are instructed to praise God no matter where you are or what you are doing. Praising God should be a lifestyle for you. "As the refining pot for silver and the furnace for gold [bring forth all the impurities of the metal], so let a man be in his trial of praise [ridding himself of all that is base or insincere; for a man is judged by what he praises and of what he boasts]." (Proverbs 27:21 AMP)

If your heart is filled with gratitude and you praise God continually, you will cleanse yourself of spiritual impurities that can block you from hearing God's voice. If you praise God and thank Him continually instead of being discouraged by adversity, you will experience "...beauty instead of ashes, the oil of joy instead of mourning, the garment [expressive] of praise instead of a heavy, burdened, and failing spirit..." (Isaiah 61:3 AMP)

Praise God continually regardless of what is happening to you. Thank God continually. Change the ashes in your life to beauty. Instead of mourning and being depressed, your heart will be filled with joy. If you praise God continually and you trust Him completely, you will not have "a heavy, burdened and failing spirit."

Praise is the language of heaven. Everyone in heaven praises God continually. If you praise God continually here on earth, you are doing what God instructs you to do.

I have centered my lifestyle around praise and thanksgiving. Whenever I get into my car and turn on the ignition, recorded praise and worship music immediately begins to play. When I drive my car, I praise God and thank Him continually. I have a substantial collection of praise and worship music that I listen to at all times when I am driving and no one else is in the car with me.

I also praise God and thank Him at night at the end of a busy day. Over the years Judy and I have developed a large collection of praise and worship videos. We have approximately 100 Gaither praise and worship videos. These videos are outstanding (see www.gaither.com).

We also have obtained many additional praise and worship videos from other sources. I watch these Southern gospel praise and worship videos most nights. Judy often joins me. As we watch and listen to these videos, we enter into praise and worship ourselves.

The recorded music in my car and the videos that we watch at night provide a constant atmosphere to praise God continually. Both of us are very grateful to God for everything in our lives.

In the remainder of this chapter and the next chapter we will study some of the things that God's Word says about the relationship between consistently praising God, thanking God and coming into His presence. There is no better place to hear God's voice than when you are in His presence. "Enter into his gates with thanksgiving, and into his courts with praise: be thankful unto him, and bless his name." (Psalm 100:4 KJV)

This verse explains that you draw closer to God when you thank Him and that you actually come into His presence when you praise Him continually. You thank God for all that He has done. You praise Him for Who He is. A constant heartfelt offering of praise and thanksgiving will bring you into God's supernatural presence.

Is your heart filled with gratitude? *Do* you spontaneously praise God and thank Him throughout every day and night of your life? "Let us come before His presence with thanksgiving; let us make a joyful noise to Him with songs of praise!" (Psalm 95:2 AMP)

Once again God explains that you come before His presence when you thank Him. This verse emphasizes *singing* your praise to God. There is something about singing when you praise God and worship Him that definitely brings you into His presence. "Blessed (happy, fortunate, to be envied) are those who dwell in Your house and Your presence; they will be singing Your praises all the day long…." (Psalm 84:4 AMP)

The words "dwell in Your house" in this verse indicate God's desire for you to remain in His presence. When you dwell in a place, you live there permanently. Each time that you come into God's presence, you will have more and more desire to come into His presence again and to remain in His presence. "Make a joyful noise to the Lord, all you lands! Serve the Lord with gladness! Come before His presence with singing!" (Psalm 100:1-2 AMP)

Once again the emphasis is placed on coming into God's presence through *singing*. Your mouth should open every day and night of your life to thank God, to praise God and to sing praise to God because your heart overflows with gratitude to Him. There is no question that your Father wants you to sing your praises to Him continually. "Sing praises to God, sing praises! Sing praises to our King, sing praises!" (Psalm 47:6 AMP)

We often explain that God emphasizes through repetition. When God tells you *four* times in one short verse of Scripture to *sing* your praises to Him, you can be certain that this is exactly what your Father wants you to do.

In this chapter we have studied Scripture that explains the relationship between praising God, thanking God and coming into His presence. There is *no* better place to hear God speaking to you than to be in His presence. In the next chapter we will study additional Scripture references pertaining to the presence of God.

Chapter 19

Be Calm, Quiet and Confident within Yourself

If you want to hear the voice of another person clearly, doesn't it make sense that the best place to hear what this person is saying is to be in the presence of this person? Hearing God's voice is no different. If you learn how to come into God's presence, you will place yourself in a spiritual position where you will continually hear what God is saying to you.

There is nothing in the spiritual realm that is greater than the awesome gift that all Christians have been given to actually come into the presence of Almighty God. "The earth trembled, the heavens also poured down [rain] at the presence of God; yonder Sinai quaked at the presence of God, the God of Israel." (Psalm 68:8 AMP)

This verse says that the earth actually trembled and that rain poured down from heaven because of the presence of God. An earthquake took place on Mt. Sinai because of the presence of God. The magnitude of the privilege of being able to enter into God's awesome presence is beyond the limits of our human comprehension. The shed blood of Jesus Christ has given you the opportunity to come into the presence of God.

Do not take lightly the wonderful opportunity that *you* have been given to enter into God's presence and to hear Him speaking to you. The psalmist David said, "You have said, Seek My face [inquire for and require My presence as your vital need]. My heart says to You, Your face (Your presence), Lord, will I seek, inquire for, and require [of necessity and on the authority of Your Word]." (Psalm 27:8 AMP)

God instructed David to seek His face and to *require* His presence as a "vital need." Coming into God's presence is not a nice to have – it is a have to have. The amplification explains that David would seek God and His presence "of necessity and on the authority of His Word." David said, "…in Your presence is fullness of joy, at Your right hand there are pleasures forevermore." (Psalm 16:11 AMP)

You cannot begin to comprehend with the limitations of your human understanding the supernatural joy that will flood your heart when you are in the presence of God. Your heart will sing with joy if you consistently turn away from the things of the world to come into God's presence. "…You will enrapture me [diffusing my soul with joy] with and in Your presence." (Acts 2:28 AMP)

The word "enrapture" consists of two parts – "en" and "rapture." The prefix "en" means "in." The word "rapture" means to be carried away with joy. You will be carried away with joy if you consistently come into the presence of God. The Bible says that "…times of refreshing (of recovering from the effects of heat, of reviving with fresh air) may come from the presence of the Lord" (Acts 3:19 AMP)

You know how you feel when you come into an air-conditioned room after you have been outside in hot and humid weather. You know how you feel when you suddenly come into fresh air after being in stale air. You will be *completely refreshed* if you consistently turn away from everything in this lost and dying world to come into the glorious presence of God. "Seek the Lord and His strength; yearn for and seek His face and to be in His presence continually!" (I Chronicles 16:11 AMP)

Please note the words "yearn" and "continually" in this verse. You should *yearn* to come into God's presence and to remain there. God would not have instructed you to live in His presence *continually* if doing this was not possible. Very few Christians live in God's presence continually.

Have a deep and sincere desire to hear God's voice continually. There is no better place to hear what God is saying to you than to be in His presence. "Humble yourselves [feeling very insignificant] in the presence of the Lord, and He will exalt you [He will lift you up and make your lives significant]." (James 4:10 AMP)

You will be very humble when you are in the presence of God. You will feel very insignificant because you are in the awesome presence of Almighty God. When you truly are humble because of the gift of coming into God's presence that you did not earn and do not deserve, God will exalt you. He will lift you up.

God will make your life meaningful and significant. He will speak to you constantly. Great things will happen in your life if you hear God speaking to you continually.

Many of the scriptural instructions that must be obeyed to hear God's voice also are required to enter into God's presence. At this time we will not go into additional instruction on how to enter into God's presence. This a separate subject that would require many chapters.

Our next book is tentatively titled *Come into the Presence of God*. We hope to have this book in print within six months of the publication of *You Can Hear God's Voice*. Depending on when you read this book, the book on God's presence should be available soon or might already be in print. Please check our website: www.lamplight.net.

In the interim, if you would like additional scriptural instructions on entering into God's presence, we recommend our book titled *What Does God Say?*. This book contains 1,221 verses of Scripture on 83 topics. One of these topics is titled PRESENCE

OF GOD. Twelve Scripture references on the presence of God are included. Each reference is accompanied by a simple and easy-to-understand explanation.

We now are ready to study several verses of Scripture that explain the relationship between being quiet and calm deep down inside of yourself and hearing the voice of God. God speaks clearly to His children who are calm and quiet regardless of any adversity they face because they trust Him completely. If you have an agitated mind for any reason, this tension will block you from hearing God's voice.

Some Christians are too active in the world. They go here. They go there. They do this. They do that. They cannot hear what God is saying to them. "…his mind takes no rest even at night. This is also vanity (emptiness, falsity, and futility)!" (Ecclesiastes 2:23 AMP)

Christians who hear God speaking to them do not allow circumstances in the world to dominate their lives. They live their lives from the inside out, not from the outside in. In Chapter 14 you learned that God usually speaks to His children in a still, small voice. You can only hear God's still, small voice to the degree that you are quiet and calm within yourself.

You cannot force yourself to be quiet and calm. The only way that you can be calm and quiet within yourself is to program yourself with God's Word by obeying God's instructions to meditate day and night on His Word.

If you truly have a deep and sincere desire to hear God speaking to you, you should carefully study and meditate on the following verses of Scripture. These verses explain how to be quiet and calm within yourself. Jesus said, "Peace I leave with you; My [own] peace I now give and bequeath to you. Not as the world gives do I give to you. Do not let your hearts be troubled, neither let them be afraid. [Stop allowing yourselves to be agitated and disturbed; and do not permit yourselves to be fearful and intimidated and cowardly and unsettled.]" (John 14:27 AMP)

Jesus was speaking to His disciples when He spoke these words. This promise also applies to your life today. If Jesus is your Savior, you can be certain that He has given *you* His supernatural peace.

The amplification says that you should not *allow* yourself to be agitated. Do not *permit* yourself to be afraid. *You decide* if you will be at peace inside of yourself because you are receiving the supernatural peace that Jesus has given to you. Obey the advice that the apostle Paul gave to the Thessalonians when he said, "…we beg you, brethren, not to allow your minds to be quickly unsettled or disturbed or kept excited or alarmed…" (II Thessalonians 2:1-2 AMP)

If you are focusing continually on God and meditating day and night on the magnificent promises in His Word, you will not *allow* yourself to be agitated by the circumstances that you face. You will be quiet and calm. God said, "…be still, and know (recognize and understand) that I am God…" (Psalm 46:10 AMP)

Whenever you are faced with a difficult problem, we recommend that you open your mouth and say repeatedly, "Be still …. Be still … Be still … Be still … Be still … Be still …" Speak God's Word. Repeatedly say and do what God instructs you to say and do.

Your Father instructs you to be still because you *know* that He is Almighty God and because you have absolute faith that He is in complete control of every circumstance. Do not allow adversity to block you from hearing God's voice. "…be calm and cool and steady, accept and suffer unflinchingly every hardship" (II Timothy 4:5 AMP)

Please note the word "every" in this verse. Your Father wants you to be calm and quiet inside of yourself *whenever* you face adversity. He does not want you to flinch or draw back. He wants you to face all adversity with quiet confidence in Him because you know that He is with you and because you trust Him completely. "…in quietness and in confidence shall be your strength." (Isaiah 30:15 KJV)

You hear God's voice and you receive God's strength to the degree that you are quiet and calm inside of yourself because you trust God. You will block yourself from receiving God's supernatural strength and from hearing God's voice if you allow yourself to be worried, fearful and agitated because of the circumstances you face.

The strength of God is released in you, to you and through you when you are calm, quiet and confident in the face of adversity. "You will guard him and keep him in perfect and constant peace whose mind [both its inclination and its character] is stayed on You, because he commits himself to You, leans on You, and hopes confidently in You." (Isaiah 26:3 AMP)

Your Father promises that He will protect you and keep you in perfect peace at all times if your mind is *focused* on Him continually and if you *trust* Him completely. Christians who consistently hear God speaking to them are focused on Him. They trust God completely.

Does your mind focus continually on God? Does every aspect of your life revolve around your absolute certainty that God lives inside of you and that He will help you (see Psalm 1:21, Isaiah 41:13, Hebrews 2:18, 4:16, and 13:6)? Your answer to these two questions will clearly determine whether you will hear God speaking to you.

If you would like detailed scriptural instruction on how to be calm and quiet within yourself, we have written several publications that will help you. We recommend our books titled *Quiet Confidence in the Lord* and *Exchange Your Worries for God's Perfect Peace*. We also recommend our Scripture Meditation Cards that are titled *Enjoy God's Wonderful Peace* and *Freedom from Worry and Fear* and the CDs that go with each set of these Scripture cards.

Chapter 20

Final Thoughts on Hearing the Voice of God

In the previous 19 chapters we have shared many Scripture references with you pertaining to hearing the voice of God. In this final chapter we would like to share some personal experiences that we have had in hearing God's voice.

I have heard God speaking to me several times each day for many years. This is Book #26 that I have written or co-authored with Judy. From the very first Christian book that I wrote almost 30 years ago, I have taken dictation from God.

I never had any formal training as a writer. I do the same thing writing books as I do when I face any challenge in my life. I search for as many Scripture references as I can find pertaining to a specific topic. I spend a significant amount of time searching for every applicable verse of Scripture. I then organize this Scripture into subtopics that ultimately will develop into chapters. I then pray daily asking God to speak to me and through me as I write each book.

I follow the outline of Scripture that I compiled. I have absolute faith that God will speak to me and through me to develop the book. We normally do six drafts of each book. I write the first two drafts. Judy then joins me in writing the next two drafts. I then write the final two drafts.

As I told you in Chapter 14, I have heard God speak to me in an audible voice only once when He told me exactly where He wanted me to live. I am still in awe to know that we are living in the home that definitely was selected for us by God.

I would like to tell you another interesting story of how I heard God's voice and how God confirmed that I had heard Him. Four and a half years ago, the dog that Judy and I had suddenly became sick and died. Judy was preparing to leave for a trip two days later. I asked Judy if she thought there was any way we could get another dog before she left.

That night Judy and I went online and looked at several dogs. We found one litter of dogs that we liked. Judy said that she would drive to that dog rescue place the next day. If she liked any of the dogs, she would bring the dog back and we could decide before she left on her trip.

After Judy left that day, I thought about what I would like to name our new dog. I would like to have named the dog Jesus, but I knew I could not do that. God spoke to me quietly and told me to name the dog J.C., the initials standing for Jesus Christ.

God cares about the little details in our lives just as loving parents care about the little things in the lives of their children. I knew that I had heard from God. I felt very good about this name for our new dog.

Judy knew nothing of this event. She was 30 miles away. She called to tell me about the dog that she liked best. Judy described this dog in some detail. I asked if the dog had a name. Judy said that the dog was named J.C.

I was absolutely amazed to know that this dog *already* was named J.C. I was certain then that this was the dog that God had for us. The people at the dog rescue place had named the dog after a musical group named J.C. I named him after Jesus Christ. I now would like to ask Judy to share a very interesting story of an occasion when she clearly heard the voice of God.

Judy says, "In 1997 I was attending a yearly missions conference at our church where I represented Lamplight Ministries. At the noon luncheon I usually met with missionaries to give Lamplight books to take back to their countries. I heard within myself, 'Don't go to the luncheon today.' I thought this was very strange, but I heard it very clearly. So, I headed for my car. I ran into Pastor Ebenezer from India face to face.

"Pastor Ebenezer had visited this church the day before and asked if he could attend the conference. He was told that there were enough people from India and not to come. He was shocked when he left. The next day as he was driving his rented car by the church, he heard within himself, 'Turn into the driveway.' He thought, 'Why would I turn in there?' Nevertheless he turned into the driveway, parked, and got out of his car. That was when we bumped into each other.

"We were both surprised. I gave Pastor Ebenezer some of our books. We knew that God had something planned for India Gospel Fellowship (see www.igf.com) and Lamplight Ministries. There is a lot more to this adventure that you can find on our website.

"Pastor Ebenezer read *Trust God for Your Finances* on the flight home to India. He then translated it into the Tamil language. Two years later I traveled to India for the first time. Since then I have made six more trips to India. I consider IGF my second home. God provided the funds for the translation to be printed and distributed. I participated in the pastors' conference where the Tamil translation was distributed.

"Countless lives have been blessed because two people heard the voice of God and obeyed His instructions. Two families, two ministries and two countries have been knit together for their joy and God's glory."

The stories about our home, our dog and Pastor Ebenezer are clear indications of hearing the voice of God. I now would like to share additional comments regarding the thousands of times I have heard God's voice over the years.

I can tell you from many years of experience that God often speaks to me at unlikely times. God has spoken to me many times just before I was about to drop off to sleep, when I was taking a shower, when my face was covered with shaving lather, when I was driving my car or when I was doing some other routine task. I have found through experience that God often speaks at a time when writing down what He says is not easy to do.

If I can give you one bit of advice above all else about hearing God's voice, that advice would be to *instantly write down* whatever God is saying to you. If you are sleepy and about to drop off to sleep and God speaks to you, get up and write down what God said. If you are taking a shower, get out of the shower and write down what God told you. If you are shaving, write it down. No matter what you are doing, I urge you to instantly write down what God says.

I have learned that, if I do not immediately write down what God tells me, this thought soon will fade away. I have learned from experience that this thought seldom comes back at a later time. Hearing God's voice is *very* important. Do *not* put off writing down what God says to you.

I have learned the hard way the frustration of hearing God speak to me and losing this precious information because I did not immediately write down what He said. After this happened a few times, I made the decision to *always* write down immediately what God says to me, no matter how inconvenient doing this might be.

God has spoken to me many times just before I was about to drop off to sleep. At this time, it would be easy not to write down what God has said because I am tired and I want to sleep. No matter how tired I am, if God speaks to me, I turn on the light. I immediately write down what God said.

I keep pads and pens all over our house. There are pads and pens in the family room and in the living room. I always have pads next to my bed. I have several pads on my desk, in the bathroom and in my car. I have learned over the years to have pads available at every conceivable place where God could speak to me.

For many years I have carried a small leather memo pad and pen. I never leave the house without this pad and pen. The pad and pen go with me at all times just as my car keys, wallet and moneyclip go with me. I would not think of leaving our home without this pad and pen.

Another time that I have learned over the years to hear God's voice is when I have lost or misplaced something. Once again, God's love for you is incredible. He cares about every little detail in your life. Whenever I lose or misplace something, I stay calm. I say something like, "Dear Father, You know exactly where this object is. I trust You completely. Please show me where this object is. Thank You, dear Father, in the name of Jesus Christ."

I have done this many times over the years. God inevitably tells me where the missing object is. He often does not tell me as soon as I would like. I then calmly go on with my life, trusting God's timing just as I trust Him in every other area.

This final chapter does not contain any Scripture or any major concepts. Just the opposite. We have shared many simple thoughts that are applicable to your everyday life. We are both very grateful for the many times that God has spoken to us. We hope that the thoughts in this chapter and the Scripture references in the preceding chapters will help you to hear God's voice.

Conclusion

We invite you to go back and read this book again. If you have not already followed our previous suggestions, we advise you to highlight or underline key scriptural thoughts pertaining to hearing God's voice. If you do, you will have identified the Scripture that is most important to you for future study and meditation.

Your Father has instructed you to meditate day and night on His Word. If you yearn to hear God's voice every day and night, we advise you to pay the definite price to study and meditate every day on these specific instructions that God has given to you.

God created you in His image. The more that you hear God's voice and the more you obey His instructions, the more Godlike you will become.

We pray that this book has helped you to hear God's voice. Please pray about sharing a copy of this book to help other people hear God's voice.

The prices of our books are as low as we can make them. We also offer quantity discounts. The order form in the back of this book explains these discounts. We desire to help as many people with the Word of God as we possibly can.

If this book has helped you, would you share your testimony with us so that we can share with others what you have learned about hearing God's voice? We normally need three to four paragraphs in a testimony so that we can consolidate this information into one solid paragraph for our newsletter and our website. Your comments will encourage many people, including the pastors and leaders in Third World countries and the inmates in prisons and jails who receive our books free of charge.

Please send any comments to lamplightmin@ yahoo.com. You can call 1-800-540-1597 and leave a message for Judy. You also can mail your comments to:

Jack and Judy Hartman
PO Box 1307
Dunedin, FL 34697

We invite you to visit our website: www.lamplight.net. You will find many comments from people who have been helped by our books. You also will find a section on biblical health as well as recipes that Judy adds each month to bless you. We are in excellent overall health at ages 81 and 73. I believe that I would not be alive today if it were not for Judy's knowledge and wisdom regarding health and her amazing recipes.

We have been blessed to share with you the results of many hours of effort that we have invested to help you to hear God speaking to you. We would be so pleased to hear from you.

Blessed to be a blessing. (Genesis 12:1-3)

Jack and Judy

Appendix

This book is filled with instructions and promises from God. However, if you have not received Jesus Christ as your Savior, you *cannot understand* the scriptural truths that are contained in this book. "…the mind of the flesh [with its carnal thoughts and purposes] is hostile to God, for it does not submit itself to God's Law; indeed it cannot." (Romans 8:7 AMP)

Please notice the word "cannot" in this verse of Scripture. If Jesus is not your Savior, you cannot understand and obey God's instructions.

People who have not received Jesus Christ as their Savior are not open to the specific instructions that God has given to us in the Bible. "…the natural, nonspiritual man does not accept or welcome or admit into his heart the gifts and teachings and revelations of the Spirit of God, for they are folly (meaningless nonsense) to him; and he is incapable of knowing them [of progressively recognizing, understanding, and becoming better acquainted with them] because they are spiritually discerned and estimated and appreciated." (I Corinthians 2:14 AMP)

The words "does not accept or welcome or admit into his heart the gifts and teachings and revelations of the Spirit of God" in this verse of Scripture are very important. Some people are strongly opposed to the Bible and what it teaches. They look at Scripture references from the Bible as "meaningless nonsense." These people are incapable of learning great spiritual truths from God until and unless they receive Jesus Christ as their Savior.

At the close of this Appendix we will explain exactly what you should do to receive Jesus Christ as your Savior. If and when you make this decision, the glorious supernatural truths of the Bible will open up to you. Jesus said, "…To you it has been given to know the secrets and mysteries of the kingdom of heaven, but to them it has not been given." (Matthew 13:11 AMP)

Jesus was speaking to *you* when He said that you can "know the secrets and mysteries of the kingdom of heaven." You must not miss out on the glorious privilege that is available to every believer to know and understand the ways of God.

A spiritual veil blocks all unbelievers from understanding the things of God. "…even if our Gospel (the glad tidings) also be hidden (obscured and covered up with a veil that hinders the knowledge of God), it is hidden [only] to those who are perishing and obscured [only] to those who are spiritually dying and veiled [only] to those who are lost." (II Corinthians 4:3 AMP)

When and if you receive Jesus Christ as your Savior, this spiritual veil is pulled aside. "…whenever a person turns [in repentance] to the Lord, the veil is stripped off and taken away." (II Corinthians 3:16 AMP)

If you obey the scriptural instructions at the end of this Appendix, Jesus Christ will become your Savior. Everything in your life will become fresh and new. "…if any person is [ingrafted] in Christ (the Messiah) he is a new creation (a new creature altogether); the old [previous moral and spiritual condition] has passed away. Behold, the fresh and new has come!" (II Corinthians 5:17 AMP)

Instead of being opposed to the teachings of the holy Bible, you will be completely open to these teachings. You will have a hunger and thirst to continually learn more supernatural truths from the Word of God. "…I endorse and delight in the Law of God in my inmost self [with my new nature]." (Romans 7:22 AMP)

Every person who has not received Jesus Christ as his or her Savior is a sinner who is doomed to live throughout eternity in the horror of hell. God has made it possible for *you* to escape this terrible eternal penalty. "…God so loved the world, that he gave his only begotten Son, that whosoever believeth in him should not perish, but have everlasting life." (John 3:16 KJV)

God knew that everyone who lived on earth after Adam and Eve would be a sinner because of the sins of Adam and Eve (see Romans 3:10-12). He sent His only Son to take upon Himself the sins of the world as He died a horrible death by crucifixion. If you believe that Jesus Christ paid the full price for *your* sins and if you trust Him completely for your eternal salvation, you will live with Him eternally in the glory of heaven.

There is only *one* way for you to live eternally in heaven after you die – that is to receive eternal salvation through Jesus Christ. "Jesus saith unto him, I am the way, the truth, and the life: no man cometh unto the Father, but by me." (John 14:6 KJV)

If you trust in anyone or anything except Jesus Christ for your eternal salvation, you will not live eternally in heaven. If you are reading these truths about living eternally in heaven because of the price that Jesus Christ has paid for you, you must understand that the same God Who created you actually is drawing you to come to Jesus Christ for eternal salvation. Jesus said, "No one is able to come to Me unless the Father Who sent Me attracts and draws him and gives him the desire to come to Me…" (John 6:44 AMP)

Are you interested in these spiritual truths about where you will live throughout eternity? If you are, you can be certain that the same awesome God Who created you is drawing *you* to Jesus Christ at this very moment.

Heaven is a glorious place. Everyone in heaven is perfectly healthy and very happy. "…God shall wipe away all tears from their eyes; and there shall be no more death, neither sorrow, nor crying, neither shall there be any more pain: for the former things are passed away. (Revelation 21:4 KJV)

All of the problems of earth will disappear when you arrive in heaven. No one in heaven dies. No one in heaven is sad. No one in heaven cries. No one in heaven suffers from pain.

You will live eternally in one place or another when you die. If you do not receive Jesus Christ as your Savior, you will live eternally in hell. People in hell will experience continual torment throughout eternity. "…the smoke of their torment ascendeth up for ever and ever: and they have no rest day nor night…" (Revelation 14:11 KJV)

Everyone in heaven is filled with joy. Everyone in hell is miserable. Jesus described what hell would be like when He said, "…there will be weeping and wailing and grinding of teeth. (Matthew 13:42 AMP)

Throughout eternity the inhabitants of hell will weep and wail. They will grind their teeth in anguish. Can you imagine living this way for the endless trillions of years of eternity? This is exactly what will happen to *you* if you reject Jesus Christ as your Savior.

How do you receive eternal salvation through Jesus Christ? "…if you acknowledge and confess with your lips that Jesus is Lord and in your heart believe (adhere to, trust in, and rely on the truth) that God raised Him from the dead, you will be saved. For with the heart a person believes (adheres to, trusts in, and relies on Christ) and so is justified (declared righteous, acceptable to God), and with the mouth he confesses (declares openly and speaks out freely his faith) and confirms [his] salvation." (Romans 10:9-10 AMP)

You must *believe in your heart* (not just think in your mind) that Jesus paid the full price for all of your sins when He was crucified. You must believe that God raised Jesus from the dead. You must open your mouth and *speak this truth* that you believe in your heart. If you believe in your heart that Jesus Christ died and rose again from the dead and that the price for your sins has been paid for and you tell others that you believe this great spiritual truth, you *have* been saved. You *will* live eternally in heaven.

If Jesus Christ was not your Savior when you began to read this book, we pray that He is your Savior now. Your life will change immensely. You will never be the same again. Every aspect of your life will be gloriously new.

Please let us know if you have become a child of God by receiving eternal salvation through Jesus Christ. We would like to pray for you and welcome you as our new Christian brother or sister. We love you and bless you in the name of our Lord Jesus Christ.

We would be so pleased to hear from you. If you are already a believer, we would be pleased to hear from you as well. We invite you to visit our website at www.lamplight.net. Please let us know if this book or one or more of our other publications has made a difference in our life. Please give us your comments so that we can share these comments in our newsletters and on our website to encourage other people.

Study Guide

What Did You Learn From This Book?

The questions in this Study Guide are carefully arranged to show you how much you have learned about hearing the voice of God. This Study Guide is not intended to be an academic test. The sole purpose of the following questions is to help you increase your practical knowledge pertaining to hearing the voice of God.

Page Reference

1. The Bible gives several instances of God speaking to people. Why should you believe that He also is speaking to you today? (Malachi 3:6 and Acts 10:34) 35

2. Is God too busy to be able to talk to people individually? Can He talk to billions of people throughout the world at the same time ? (Ephesians 4:6, Exodus 15:11, Jeremiah 32:17 and Amos 4:13) 35-36

3. How can you be certain that God knows every minute detail about you when He is speaking to you? (Psalm 139:1-4 and Hebrews 4:13) 36-37

4. Why would the same awesome God Who created heaven and earth want to talk with you individually every day of your life? (Psalm 8:3-4) 37

5. Why are unbelievers unable to hear the voice of God? (Isaiah 59:2) 39

6. How can you be certain that, if Jesus Christ is your Savior, you can hear God speaking to you? (II Corinthians 5:17, Hebrews 8:12, John 8:47 and Matthew 13:11) 39-40

7. What does the Bible say about how often God speaks to you? (Job 33:14) 40

8. There is no question that God wants to speak to you. Why do you need to learn how to hear His voice? (Revelation 3:20, Matthew 11:15 and Matthew 13:9) 40-41

9. Why should you pay careful attention to what you allow to come into your ears? Why does your ability to hear God's voice increase progressively? (Mark 4:24) 41

10. If Jesus Christ is your Savior, how can you be certain that God Himself is your loving Father? (II Corinthians 6:18, Ephesians 2:19, I John 3:1, John 1:12-13, Ephesians 2:15 and Galatians 3:26) 43-44

11. If Jesus Christ is your Savior, how can you be certain the Holy Spirit lives in your heart? (Galatians 4:6) 44

12. God very much wants you to listen to what He is saying to you. How important is it for you to hear what God is saying to you? (Psalm 81:13 and Job 23:12) 44-45

13. What does the Bible say about God's love for you? Why is your knowledge of God's love for you important in relation to hearing His voice? (Lamentations 1:22-23, John 17:23, Ephesians 3:17-19 and Isaiah 54:10).... 47-48

14. Why should you have good reason to believe that God often will encourage you when He speaks to you? (Romans 15:4-5 and II Corinthians 7:6) 48

15. What does the Bible say about God teaching you when

	He talks to you? (John 5:30, John 6:45, Isaiah 48:17, Isaiah 50:4 and Psalm 32:8) 49
16.	Why should you praise God and thank Him for teaching you? (Psalm 119:171) 49
17.	Jesus Christ is our example in every area of our lives. What does Jesus say about the importance of being taught by His Father? How does this statement apply to your life today? (John 8:28) 50
18.	What does the Bible say about God guiding you throughout your life? (Isaiah 30:20-21, Psalm 48:14, Psalm 37:23 and Psalm 73:23-24) 51-52
19.	What does the Bible say about God directing your steps? (Proverbs 16:9) 52
20.	How often will God guide you? (Isaiah 58:11) 52
21.	What does the Bible teach about God speaking to you when you face adversity? (Job 36:15) 52
22.	Can you expect God to speak through you and give you the words you have to have when you need them? (Exodus 4:12, Proverbs 16:1 and Matthew 10:19-20) 53
23.	What does the Bible instruct you to do when you need wisdom from God? (James 1:5) 54
24.	What does the Bible say in regard to the Holy Spirit knowing about the future? Will He share this information with you? (John 16:13) 54
25.	What is the relationship between expecting God to speak to you and actually hearing His voice? (Hebrews 3:12, Matthew 8:13, Psalm 27:14 and Psalm 85:8) 56
26.	How does the biblical story of God speaking to a young boy named Samuel apply to your ability to hear God speaking to you? (I Samuel 3:3-10) 56-57

27. What does God promise to His children who faithfully listen every day for His voice? (Proverbs 8:33-34 and Isaiah 55:3) 57-58

28. God wants each of His children to learn how to hear His voice. What does He promise to do throughout every day of your life if you expect to hear Him speaking to you and if you do everything you can to learn and obey His instructions pertaining to hearing His voice? (II Chronicles 16:9, Jeremiah 33:3, Proverbs 4:13) 58-59

29. How can you be certain that the voice you are hearing is the voice of God? How does the biblical analogy of a sheep and the voice of its shepherd apply to your certainty that you are hearing God's voice? (John 10:2-5 and 10:27) 61-62

30. You know the voices of people who are close to you. Why is it important for you to continually draw closer to God instead of having a distant relationship with Him or no relationship at all if you sincerely desire to hear His voice? (Job 36:26 and Mark 7:6) 63

31. What does the Bible say about Jesus Christ giving you the privilege to progressively know God more intimately? (I John 5:20) 64

32. What are you instructed to do so that God will come close to you? (James 4:8) 64

33. How do you become one with God and therefore hear His voice much more clearly? (I Corinthians 6:17 and Deuteronomy 13:4) 65

34. The Bible instructs you to be zealous to know the Lord. What does the word "zealous" mean? How does this instruction apply to your relationship with the Lord? (Hosea 6:3 and Hebrews 11:6) 65

35. What does the Bible mean when you are instructed to abide in God? Do these words describe your relationship

	with God? (I John 2:27)	65
36.	What provision has God made for you to escape from the moral decay that pervades the world today? (II Peter 1:4)	67
37.	What does the Bible say about God being the Author of the Bible? Why did God inspire the Bible? (II Timothy 3:16-17)	68
38.	The Word of God is filled with the supernatural power of God. How is this supernatural power released in your life? (Hebrews 4:12 and I Thessalonians 2:13)	68
39.	What did Jesus Christ say about the relationship between your knowledge of the Bible and your ability to hear His voice? (John 18:37)	69
40.	Everything in the world is temporary. How can you be certain that the Bible is eternal? (Matthew 24:35 and I Peter 1:23)	69
41.	What does the word "sanctification" mean? Why should you consistently sanctify yourself so that you will hear what God is saying to you? (John 17:17, John 8:32 and Romans 8:7-8)	69-70
42.	What did Jesus tell the Pharisees about why they did not hear God's voice? How does this comment apply to your life? (John 5:37-38)	70
43.	Why did God tell you that you should tremble at His Word? How does reverence for the Word of God affect your ability to hear God's voice? (Psalm 119:161, Proverbs 13:13, Isaiah 66:2 and Isaiah 66:5)	73-74
44.	What is the relationship between consistently studying the Bible and understanding the ways of God that are very different and very much higher than the ways of the world? (Isaiah 55:8-9)	74
45.	What are you instructed to do in regard to the price that	

	you pay when you study the Bible? (II Timothy 2:15) 74
46.	How will your life be changed if you consistently renew your mind in the Word of God? (Romans 12:2) 75
47.	How frequently should you renew your mind by studying the Word of God? (Ephesians 4:22-24 and II Corinthians 4:16) 75
48.	What is the relationship between understanding the ways of God and consistently studying and meditating on the Word of God? (Psalm 119:130) 76
49.	Why is it important for you to continually store up the Word of God in your mind and your heart? (Deuteronomy 11:18, Colossians 3:16 and Deuteronomy 30:14) 76-77
50.	How often did the psalmist meditate on the Word of God? (Psalm 119:97) 77
51.	What did God instruct Joshua to do when he succeeded Moses as the leader of Israel? What did God promise if Joshua obeyed these instructions? How does this promise apply to your life today, particularly in regard to your ability to hear the voice of God? (Joshua 1:8) 77
52.	The Bible says that, if you delight in the Word of God and meditate day and night on the Word of God, you will be like a tree that is planted next to a stream of water. How does this analogy apply to the blessings that you will receive if you meditate day and night on the Word of God? (Psalm 1:2-3) 78
53.	What does God promise to His children who consistently obey the instructions in His Word and seek Him wholeheartedly? (Psalm 119:2) 81
54.	What is the relationship between becoming better acquainted with God and obeying His instructions? (I John 2:3-4) 81-82

55. The Bible instructs you to walk uprightly. What does the word "uprightly" mean? What is the relationship between walking uprightly and hearing God's voice? (Psalm 84:11) 82

56. What is the relationship between consistently obeying God's instructions, seeking God's will for your life, and hearing the voice of God? (I John 3:22) 82

57. What does the Bible say about Christians who place themselves in a spiritual position to be deceived by Satan and the relationship between doing what the Word of God says instead of just listening to its instructions? (James 1:22) 82

58. What does God promise if you will consistently obey the instructions that He gives you in His Word? (Exodus 19:5 and Deuteronomy 28:1-2) 83

59. What does the Bible say about the relationship between the food that you eat and living in obedience to God's instructions? (Deuteronomy 8:3) 83

60. What does God promise to you if you carefully listen to His voice and obey His instructions? (Deuteronomy 15:4-5 and Jeremiah 7:23) 83-84

61. What is the relationship between having a humble and teachable heart and hearing the voice of God? (Hebrews 3:15) 84

62. How do you show your love for God? (I John 5:3) 84

63. What is the relationship between the length and quality of your life and loving God, obeying God's voice and clinging to God continually? (Deuteronomy 30:20) 84

64. God wants to reveal great hidden truths to you. What is the relationship between learning these truths and your ability to hear God's voice? (Mark 4:22-23) 85

65. What is the relationship between your spiritual maturity and consistently hearing the voice of God? (Luke 8:18 and Hebrews 5:11-12) 85

66. What does the Bible say about heaven being your real home if Jesus Christ is your Savior? Why should you consistently turn away from things in the world? (Philippians 3:20, Psalm 119:18-19, John 15:19 and I Peter 2:11) 87-88

67. What influence can Satan and his demons have on your ability to hear God? (Ephesians 5:15-16 and I John 5:19) 88

68. What is the relationship between turning away from external and superficial things in the world and being able to hear God speaking to you? (Romans 12:2, I Samuel 12:20-21, II Timothy 3:4, I Timothy 6:20, I John 2:15-16 and Colossians 2:20) 89-90

69. Where should your focus be instead of focusing on things in the world? Why should you consistently separate yourself from unbelievers if you truly desire to hear what God is saying to you? (Colossians 3:2 and II Corinthians 6:17) 91

70. What did Jesus do when a large crowd came to Him to be healed that clearly indicated the importance He placed on quiet time with God? Why should what Jesus did here affect the priorities in your life? (Luke 5:15-16 and Luke 6:12) 93-94

71. What principle did Jesus explain in the story about Mary and Martha that applies to your life today and your ability to hear God's voice? (Luke 10:38-42) 94

72. The Bible instructs you to pursue consecration and holiness and to sanctify yourself. What do these words mean? How do these instructions apply to your life today and your ability to hear God speaking to you?

	(Hebrews 12:14 and Joshua 3:5)	95
73.	Why should your daily quiet time with God be a necessity, not an option? (I Chronicles 22:19 and Psalm 23:2-3)	95
74.	The Bible refers several times to quiet time with God in the morning. Why is quiet time in the morning, as opposed to other times in the day, especially important? (Mark 1:35, Job 7:17-18, Psalm 5:3, Psalm 143:8 and 119:148)	96-97
75.	Some people find that they are lonely when they first begin setting aside quiet time to be with God each day. What did Jesus Christ say about this subject? (John 16:32)	98
76.	When you hear the voice of God, are you normally hearing God speak to you from His throne in heaven? (Jeremiah 23:23)	99
77.	If Jesus Christ is your Savior, how can you be certain that God lives in your heart and that He speaks from within you? (Ephesians 4:6, Zephaniah 3:17 and Luke 17:21)	99-100
78.	Who is the hidden person of the heart? How does your awareness of this hidden person affect your ability to hear God? (I Peter 3:4)	98
79.	What did Jesus say about the importance of focusing continually on the indwelling presence of God and the result that doing this will have in your life? (John 14:10)	100
80.	Can you be certain that God is with you at all times? Will He ever leave you or forsake you? (Genesis 28:15, Joshua 1:5 and Joshua 1:9)	101
81.	In addition to God living in your heart, how can you know that Jesus also lives in your heart and that the Holy Spirit lives in your heart? Why should every aspect	

of your life revolve around your absolute certainty that God, Jesus Christ and the Holy Spirit live in your heart? (Acts 17:28, Ephesians 3:17, I Corinthians 3:16 and Colossians 2:10) 101-102

82. What does the Bible say about certain instances when the voice of God was supernaturally loud? (Job 37:2-4, John 12:29 and Ezekiel 43:2) 103

83. When God speaks to you, does He usually speak in a loud voice? Does God often speak audibly to you? (I Kings 19:12) 104

84. What does the Bible say about how Satan spoke to Jesus in an attempt to influence Him? (Matthew 4:1-4) 107

85. What does the Bible say about Satan speaking directly to Judas Iscariot in an attempt to influence him? What was the result of Satan speaking to Judas? (John 13:2) 107

86. Satan and his demons are still in the atmosphere around the world. They have not gone anywhere. Satan's demons will speak to you, trying to influence you. How can you tell whether what you are hearing comes from Satan's demons or from God? (John 8:44) 108

87. What relationship does the amount of the Word of God that is stored up in your heart have on identifying the voices of Satan's demons and not being influenced by what they say? (I John 2:14, Psalm 17:4 and John 10:10) 108-109

88. What happened to the Israelites when they refused to listen to God? How does this principle apply to your life today? (Psalm 81:11-12 and Hebrews 12:25) 111-112

89. What is the relationship between doing what the Word of God instructs you to do and doing what seems right to you based on human wisdom and logic? How does

the answer to this question influence your ability to hear the voice of God? (Proverbs 14:12 and I Corinthians 3:19-20) 112

90. Many people make decisions based on traditional worldly thinking and block themselves from hearing the voice of God. What did Jesus say to a group of Pharisees about the effect that traditional thinking has on the Word of God? (Mark 7:9 and Mark 7:13) 112-113

91. Why does pride block people from hearing the voice of God? (I Peter 5:5) 113

92. What does the Bible say about consistently fearing and revering God and hearing His voice and having a hard heart and not hearing God's voice? (Proverbs 28:14, Hebrews 3:7-8 and Hebrews 4:7) 114

93. What is the relationship between you having a humble heart and hearing God speaking to you? (Psalm 138:6, Proverbs 3:34, Proverbs 14:6 and Psalm 25:9) 117

94. If you are not hearing the voice of God and you consistently pray to God asking Him to teach you how to hear His voice, what effect will these prayers of faith have in your life? (Proverbs 15:8 and John 15:7) 118

95. What is the relationship between God being in first place in your life ahead of anyone or anything else and hearing God's voice? (Exodus 20:3, Matthew 6:33, John 3:30, Colossians 1:18, Deuteronomy 4:29 and Isaiah 58:13-14) 118-119

96. What is the relationship between yielding control of your life to the Holy Spirit and hearing the voice of God? (Romans 8:9 and Galatians 5:16) 120

97. The Bible says that God created you to fear Him. What does this mean? What is the relationship between fearing God and hearing His voice? (Ecclesiastes 12:13, Psalm

33:8, Psalm 128:1, Psalm 25:14, Psalm 115:11, Psalm 25:12, Proverbs 19:23 and Proverbs 23:17) 121-123

98. What is the relationship between focusing continually on God, your life revolving around the intimacy of your relationship with God and hearing God's voice? (Psalm 25:15, Nehemiah 4:14 and Hebrews 11:27) 123

99. Why do Christians who frequently complain block themselves from hearing God speaking to them? Who are you actually complaining about whenever you complain? (Philippians 2:14) 125

100. How often should you give thanks to God? (Ephesians 5:20 and I Thessalonians 5:18) 125-126

101. What does the Bible mean when it refers to the sacrifice of praise? What does the Bible mean when it refers to an offering of praise? Why should you praise God and thank Him continually? (Hebrews 13:15 and Psalm 50:23) 126

102. What else does the Bible teach about what God created you to do in addition to creating you to fear Him? (Isaiah 43:21) 126

103. Why is God worthy of your praise? (Psalm 145:3 and Revelation 4:11) 127

104. How often should you praise the Lord? (Psalm 113:3) 127

105. What effect will consistent heartfelt praise to God have on the spiritual condition of your heart? (Proverbs 27:21 and Isaiah 61:3) 127

106. What is the relationship between a grateful heart that continually thanks and praises God and entering into God's presence? (Psalm 100:4) 128

107. What does the Bible say about singing your praise to God? (Psalm 95:2, Psalm 84:4, Psalm 100:1-2 and Psalm 47:6) 129

108. The presence of God is awesome. What does the Bible say happened to the earth, to heaven and to Mount Sinai in the presence of God? (Psalm 68:8) 131

109. God has given you the opportunity to consistently enter into His awesome presence. How important should entering into God's presence be to you? (Psalm 27:8) 132

110. What does the Bible say about the relationship between your heart being filled with joy and coming into the presence of God? (Psalm 16:11, Acts 2:28 and Acts 3:19) 132

111. How often should you seek to be in God's presence? (I Chronicles 16:11) 132

111. If you are very humble because of the awesomeness of the opportunity that you have been given to be in the presence of God, how will God react to your humility? What is the relationship between this humble attitude, being in the presence of God and your ability to hear God's voice? (James 4:10) 133

113. What is the relationship between being calm and quiet because of your confidence in the Lord and your ability to hear His voice? (Ecclesiastes 2:23, John 14:27, II Thessalonians 2:1-2, Psalm 46:10, II Timothy 4:5 and Isaiah 30:15) 134-135

114. What does God promise will happen in your life if your mind is consistently focused on Him and you trust Him completely? (Isaiah 26:3) 136

A Few Words About Lamplight Ministries, Inc.

Lamplight Ministries, Inc. originally began in 1983 as Lamplight Publications. After ten years as a publishing firm with a goal of selling Christian books, Lamplight Ministries was founded in 1993. Jack and Judy Hartman founded Lamplight Ministries with a mission of continuing to sell their publications and also to *give* large numbers of these publications free of charge to needy people all over the world.

Lamplight Ministries was created to allow people who have been blessed by our publications to share in financing the translation, printing and distribution of our books into other languages and also to distribute our publications free of charge to inmates in jails and prisons. Over the years many partners of Lamplight Ministries have shared Jack and Judy's vision. As the years have gone by, Lamplight Ministries' giving has increased with each passing year. Thousands of people in jails and prisons and in Third World countries have received our publications free of charge.

Our books and Scripture Meditation Cards have been translated into eleven foreign languages – Armenian, Danish, Greek, Hebrew, German, Korean, Norwegian, Portuguese, Russian, Spanish and the Tamil dialect in India. The translations in these languages are not available from Lamplight Ministries in the United

States. These translations can only be obtained in the countries where they have been printed.

The pastors of many churches in Third World countries have written to say that they consistently preach sermons in their churches based on the scriptural contents of our publications. We believe that people in several churches in many different countries consistently hear sermons that are based on the scriptural contents of our publications. Praise the Lord!

Jack Hartman was the sole author of twelve Christian books. After co-authoring one book with Judy, Jack and Judy co-authored ten sets of Scripture Meditation Cards. Judy has been the co-author of every subsequent book. Jack and Judy currently are working on other books that they believe the Lord is leading them to write as co-authors.

We invite you to request our newsletters to stay in touch with us, to learn of our latest publications and to read comments from people all over the world. Please write, fax, call or email us. You are very special to us. We love you and thank God for you. Our heart is to take the gospel to the world and for our books to be available in every known language. Hallelujah!

Lamplight Ministries, Inc.,

PO Box 1307 - Dunedin, Florida, 34697. USA

Phone: 1-800-540-1597 • Fax: 1-727-784-2980

website: lamplight.net • email: lamplight@lamplight.net

We offer you a substantial quantity discount

From the beginning of our ministry we have been led of the Lord to offer the same quantity discount to individuals that we offer to Christian bookstores. Each individual has a sphere of influence with a specific group of people. We believe that you know many people who need to learn the scriptural contents of our publications.

The Word of God encourages us to give freely to others. We encourage you to give selected copies of these publications to people you know who need help in the specific areas that are covered by our publications. See our order form for specific information on the quantity discounts that we make available to you so that you can share our books, Scripture Meditation Cards and CDs with others.

A request to our readers

If this book has helped you, we would like to receive your comments so that we can share them with others. Your comments can encourage other people to study our publications to learn from the scriptural contents of these publications.

When we receive a letter containing comments on any of our books, cassette tapes or Scripture Meditation Cards, we prayerfully take out excerpts from these letters. These selected excerpts are included in our newsletters and occasionally in our advertising and promotional materials.

If any of our publications have been a blessing to you, please share your comments with us so that we can share them with others. Tell us in your own words what a specific publication has meant to you and why you would recommend it to others. Please give as much specific information as possible. We prefer three or four paragraphs so that we can condense this into one paragraph.

Thank you for taking a few minutes of your time to encourage other people to learn from the scripture references in our publications.

ORDER FORM FOR BOOKS

Book Title	Quantity	Total
What Does God Say? ($18)	_____ x $18 =	_____
You Can Hear the Voice of God ($14)	_____ x $14 =	_____
Effective Prayer ($14)	_____ x $14 =	_____
God's Instructions for Growing Older ($14)	_____ x $14 =	_____
A Close and Intimate Relationship with God ($14)	_____ x $14 =	_____
God's Joy Regardless of Circumstances ($14)	_____ x $14 =	_____
Victory Over Adversity ($14)	_____ x $14 =	_____
Receive Healing from the Lord ($14)	_____ x $14 =	_____
Unshakable Faith in Almighty God ($14)	_____ x $14 =	_____
Exchange Your Worries for God's Perfect Peace ($14)	_____ x $14 =	_____
God's Wisdom is Available to You ($14)	_____ x $14 =	_____
Overcoming Fear ($14)	_____ x $14 =	_____
Trust God For Your Finances ($10)	_____ x $10 =	_____
What Will Heaven Be Like? ($10)	_____ x $10 =	_____
Quiet Confidence in the Lord ($10)	_____ x $10 =	_____
Never, Never Give Up ($10)	_____ x $10 =	_____
Increased Energy and Vitality ($10)	_____ x $10 =	_____
God's Will for Our Lives ($10)	_____ x $10 =	_____
How to Study the Bible ($7)	_____ x $7 =	_____
Nuggets of Faith ($7)	_____ x $7 =	_____
100 Years From Today ($7)	_____ x $7 =	_____

    Price of books _____

    Minus 40% discount for 5-9 books _____

    Minus 50% discount for 10 or more books _____

    Net price of order _____

    Add 15% **before discount** for shipping and handling _____

    Florida residents only, add 7% sales tax _____

    Tax deductible contribution to Lamplight Ministries, Inc. _____

Enclosed check or money order (do not send cash) _____

(Foreign orders must be submitted in U.S. dollars.)

Please make check payable to **Lamplight Ministries, Inc**. and mail to:
PO Box 1307, Dunedin, FL 34697

MC____ Visa____ AmEx____ Disc.____ Card # _____

Exp Date _____ Signature _____

Name _____

Address _____

City _____

State or Province _____ Zip or Postal Code _____

Email _____ Website: _____

ORDER FORM FOR SCRIPTURE MEDITATION CARDS AND CDs

SCRIPTURE MEDITATION CARDS	QUANTITY	PRICE
Find God's Will for Your Life ($5)	_____	_____
Financial Instructions from God ($5)	_____	_____
Freedom from Worry and Fear ($5)	_____	_____
A Closer Relationship with the Lord ($5)	_____	_____
Our Father's Wonderful Love ($5)	_____	_____
Receive Healing from the Lord ($5)	_____	_____
Receive God's Blessing in Adversity ($5)	_____	_____
Enjoy God's Wonderful Peace ($5)	_____	_____
God is Always with You ($5)	_____	_____
Continually Increasing Faith in God ($5)	_____	_____

CDs	QUANTITY	PRICE
Find God's Will for Your Life ($10)	_____	_____
Financial Instructions from God ($10)	_____	_____
Freedom from Worry and Fear ($10)	_____	_____
A Closer Relationship with the Lord ($10)	_____	_____
Our Father's Wonderful Love ($10)	_____	_____
Receive Healing from the Lord ($10)	_____	_____
Receive God's Blessing in Adversity ($10)	_____	_____
Enjoy God's Wonderful Peace ($10)	_____	_____
God is Always with You ($10)	_____	_____
Continually Increasing Faith in God ($10)	_____	_____

TOTAL PRICE _____

Minus 40% discount for 5-9 Scripture Cards and CDs _____
Minus 50% discount for 10 or more Scripture Cards and CDs _____
Net price of order _____
Add 15% **before discount** for shipping and handling _____
Florida residents only, add 7% sales tax _____
Tax deductible contribution to Lamplight Ministries, Inc. _____
Enclosed check or money order (do not send cash) _____
(Foreign orders must be submitted in U.S. dollars.)

Please make check payable to **Lamplight Ministries, Inc**. and mail to:
PO Box 1307, Dunedin, FL 34697

MC____ Visa____ AmEx____ Disc.____ Card # _____

Exp Date _____ Signature _____

Name _____

Address _____

City _____

State or Province _____ Zip or Postal Code _____

Email _____ Website: _____

ORDER FORM FOR BOOKS

Book Title	Quantity	Total
What Does God Say? ($18)	_____ x $18 =	_____
You Can Hear the Voice of God ($14)	_____ x $14 =	_____
Effective Prayer ($14)	_____ x $14 =	_____
God's Instructions for Growing Older ($14)	_____ x $14 =	_____
A Close and Intimate Relationship with God ($14)	_____ x $14 =	_____
God's Joy Regardless of Circumstances ($14)	_____ x $14 =	_____
Victory Over Adversity ($14)	_____ x $14 =	_____
Receive Healing from the Lord ($14)	_____ x $14 =	_____
Unshakable Faith in Almighty God ($14)	_____ x $14 =	_____
Exchange Your Worries for God's Perfect Peace ($14)	_____ x $14 =	_____
God's Wisdom is Available to You ($14)	_____ x $14 =	_____
Overcoming Fear ($14)	_____ x $14 =	_____
Trust God For Your Finances ($10)	_____ x $10 =	_____
What Will Heaven Be Like? ($10)	_____ x $10 =	_____
Quiet Confidence in the Lord ($10)	_____ x $10 =	_____
Never, Never Give Up ($10)	_____ x $10 =	_____
Increased Energy and Vitality ($10)	_____ x $10 =	_____
God's Will for Our Lives ($10)	_____ x $10 =	_____
How to Study the Bible ($7)	_____ x $7 =	_____
Nuggets of Faith ($7)	_____ x $7 =	_____
100 Years From Today ($7)	_____ x $7 =	_____

    Price of books   _____

    Minus 40% discount for 5-9 books   _____

    Minus 50% discount for 10 or more books   _____

    Net price of order   _____

    Add 15% **before discount** for shipping and handling   _____

    Florida residents only, add 7% sales tax   _____

    Tax deductible contribution to Lamplight Ministries, Inc.   _____

Enclosed check or money order (do not send cash)   _____

(Foreign orders must be submitted in U.S. dollars.)

Please make check payable to **Lamplight Ministries, Inc.** and mail to:
PO Box 1307, Dunedin, FL 34697

MC____ Visa____ AmEx____ Disc.____ Card # _____

Exp Date _____ Signature _____

Name _____

Address _____

City _____

State or Province _____ Zip or Postal Code _____

Email _____ Website: _____

ORDER FORM FOR SCRIPTURE MEDITATION CARDS AND CDs

SCRIPTURE MEDITATION CARDS	**QUANTITY**	**PRICE**
Find God's Will for Your Life ($5)	_____	_____
Financial Instructions from God ($5)	_____	_____
Freedom from Worry and Fear ($5)	_____	_____
A Closer Relationship with the Lord ($5)	_____	_____
Our Father's Wonderful Love ($5)	_____	_____
Receive Healing from the Lord ($5)	_____	_____
Receive God's Blessing in Adversity ($5)	_____	_____
Enjoy God's Wonderful Peace ($5)	_____	_____
God is Always with You ($5)	_____	_____
Continually Increasing Faith in God ($5)	_____	_____

CDs	**QUANTITY**	**PRICE**
Find God's Will for Your Life ($10)	_____	_____
Financial Instructions from God ($10)	_____	_____
Freedom from Worry and Fear ($10)	_____	_____
A Closer Relationship with the Lord ($10)	_____	_____
Our Father's Wonderful Love ($10)	_____	_____
Receive Healing from the Lord ($10)	_____	_____
Receive God's Blessing in Adversity ($10)	_____	_____
Enjoy God's Wonderful Peace ($10)	_____	_____
God is Always with You ($10)	_____	_____
Continually Increasing Faith in God ($10)	_____	_____

TOTAL PRICE _____

Minus 40% discount for 5-9 Scripture Cards and CDs _____
Minus 50% discount for 10 or more Scripture Cards and CDs _____
Net price of order _____
Add 15% **before discount** for shipping and handling _____
Florida residents only, add 7% sales tax _____
Tax deductible contribution to Lamplight Ministries, Inc. _____
Enclosed check or money order (do not send cash) _____
(Foreign orders must be submitted in U.S. dollars.)

Please make check payable to **Lamplight Ministries, Inc.** and mail to:
PO Box 1307, Dunedin, FL 34697

MC____ Visa____ AmEx____ Disc.____ Card # _____

Exp Date _____ Signature _____

Name _____

Address _____

City _____

State or Province _____ Zip or Postal Code _____

Email _____ Website: _____

www.ingramcontent.com/pod-product-compliance
Lightning Source LLC
LaVergne TN
LVHW051121080426
835510LV00018B/2164

Walking the Wheel of the Year Companion Workbook

WRITTEN AND ILLUSTRATED BY

EMMA-JANE CROSS

GREEN MAGIC

Walking the Wheel of the Year Companion Workbook © 2025
by Emma-Jane Cross. All rights reserved.
No part of this book may be used or reproduced in
any form without written permission of the author,
except in the case of quotations in articles and reviews.

Green Magic
53 Brooks Road
Street
Somerset
BA16 0PP
England
www.greenmagicpublishing.com

Designed & typeset by Carrigboy, Wells, Somerset, UK
www.carrigboy.co.uk

ISBN 978 1 915580 31 3

GREEN MAGIC